A FIELD GUIDE TO THE
WHALES, PORPOISES
and SEALS

A FIELD GUIDE TO THE
WHALES,
PORPOISES *and*
SEALS *of the Gulf of Maine*
and Eastern Canada
CAPE COD TO NEWFOUNDLAND

Steven K. Katona
Valerie Rough
David T. Richardson

ILLUSTRATIONS BY
John R. Quinn, D. D. Tyler,
and Sarah Landry

CHARLES SCRIBNER'S SONS · NEW YORK

Illustrations copyright © 1983 Sarah Landry, D.D. Tyler, and
John R. Quinn
Copyright © 1983 Steven K. Katona
Copyright © 1975, 1977 by Steven Katona, David Richardson

Library of Congress Cataloging in Publication Data

Katona, Steven K.
  A field guide to the whales, porpoises and seals
of the Gulf of Maine and Eastern Canada.
  Rev. ed. of: A field guide to the whales and seals of
the Gulf of Maine. 2nd ed. © 1977.
  Bibliography: p.
  Discography: p.
  Includes index.
  1. Marine mammals—Maine, Gulf of—Identification.
2. Marine mammals—Atlantic Coast (Canada)—Identification.
3. Mammals—Maine, Gulf of—Identification.   4. Mammals—
Atlantic Coast (Canada)—Identification.   I. Rough,
Valerie, 1945-   II. Richardson, David T.
III. Title.
QL713.2.K37   1983   599.5   83-3337
ISBN 0-684-17901-6 (cloth)
ISBN 0-684-17902-4 (paper)

1 3 5 7 9 11 13 15 17 19   F/C   20 18 16 14 12 10 8 6 4 2
1 3 5 7 9 11 13 15 17 19   F/P   20 18 16 14 12 10 8 6 4 2

Printed in the United States of America.

David Richardson's love of Maine's seals helped to make this book possible. His field research provided the first detailed record of the distribution and abundance of harbor and gray seals along the Maine coast. He brought to the study of marine mammals both an emotional appreciation for the animals he observed and a desire for scientific precision in recording his observations. David's accomplishments were not won easily, because he had cystic fibrosis. His will to continue learning and working was an inspiration to everyone who knew him. We dedicate this book to his memory.

Contents

Preface

THE PREVIOUS TWO EDITIONS OF THIS FIELD GUIDE CONCEN-
trated on marine mammals of the Gulf of Maine. In this third
edition, we have added several additional species that may
be encountered in subarctic Atlantic Canada, new information about whale watching or seal watching in American and
Canadian waters, and sections on large sea creatures occasionally seen by whale watchers. Throughout the book we
use the term *study area* to refer to coastal and shelf waters
between Cape Cod and southern Labrador. We elected not
to include species found only in the Canadian arctic, which
have only rarely, if ever, been reported as strays or strandings farther south than Labrador. Information on those species, namely the bowhead whale, the narwhal, and the
bearded seal, may be found in the Bibliography.

In our selection and discussion of species, we have been
guided by the desire to keep this field guide small and con-
cise. We have endeavored to include information that will
be most useful to a person observing the animals in the wild,
and have left other details to the Bibliography provided. The

guide includes drawings, photographs, and basic information on the twenty-two whales and six seals that have been seen at sea or stranded on a beach between Cape Cod and southern Labrador. The text and illustrations emphasize the importance of field marks for species identification. Field marks are outstanding color patterns, body shapes, or behavior traits that observers can use to distinguish species rapidly and accurately in the wild. As in bird watching, it pays to know the field marks of the various species well, because different whales or seals are frequently difficult to tell apart, and because often only a small part of the animal can be seen and only for a second or two. Since most whales or seals will be seen from a distance, a good binocular (7 power x 35 or 7 x 50 mm) will usually be necessary. Instruments with greater magnification can be used on land, but are hard to hold on a rocking boat. Similarly, telephoto lenses longer than about 300 mm for a 35-mm camera will require a combination of fast film speed, a chest mount or rifle mount, a steady hand, and a calm day. Telescopes cannot be used from boats, but the text suggests several locations on land where they may be used to observe whales or seals.

Watching whales or seals can provide observers with a unique and exhilarating experience. Equally important, accurate written reports or photographs by amateurs can be valuable additions to the known information on these animals, some of which are still very poorly understood. Sample sighting report forms are provided in this guide along with instructions on how to report your observations. We would be grateful to receive accounts of all sightings of living, injured, or dead whales, porpoises, and seals from the study area. Firsthand observations or newspaper accounts may be sent to us at Allied Whale, c/o College of the Atlantic, Bar Harbor, Maine 04609. We will forward information obtained from Canadian waters to interested Canadian scientists.

It is important to note that all marine mammals in U.S. waters are protected by the Marine Mammal Protection Act of 1972, and all the large whales are also protected by the Endangered Species Act of 1973. Harassment is not only detrimental to animals, but is also punishable by fines or imprisonment. Even stranded or dead specimens are protected, and special permission must be obtained to touch them. In New England, any stranded, injured, or entrapped marine mammal should be reported immediately to the local police; the coastal warden; the National Marine Fisheries Service Enforcement Division (offices in Portland, Maine, and Gloucester, Mass.); or to the New England Aquarium, Central Wharf, Boston, Mass. 02110 (617) 742-8830, which is the major clearinghouse for such data from this area. All data are submitted to Scientific Event Alert Network (SEAN), Smithsonian Institution, Washington, D.C. 20560, which is a worldwide data base for stranding information.

Acknowledgments

WE THANK JAMES G. MEAD, EDWARD D. MITCHELL, ROGER
and Katy Payne, William E. Schevill, David E. Sergeant,
William A. Watkins, and Howard E. Winn for comments,
teaching, and encouragement to create this guide. Throughout the years of preparation and updating of this book, help
given by colleagues and students at the College of the Atlan-
tic has been immeasurably valuable. In particular, we wish
to thank Lisa Baraff, Ben Baxter, Lisa Carpenter, Gayle
Cliett, Peter Cohen, Kate Darling, Steven Donoso, William
H. Drury, Samuel A. Eliot, Nancy Gunnlaugson, Matthew
Hare, Katherine Hazard, Catherine Kiorpes, Scott Kraus,
Ed Lemire, Rebecca May, Bill McDowell, Sydney Rathbun
McKay, Stephen Mullane, Cathy Ramsdell, Ann Rivers,
Sentiel Rommel, Steve Savage, Rachel Snow, Peter Stevick,
Greg Stone, Porter Turnbull, Katrina Van Dine, and Rick
Waters.

Our debt to Robin Hazard, who coauthored the first and
second editions of this guide, is great. Our interest and excitement have frequently been rekindled over the years by

observations so generously shared with us by Bob Bowman, Tudor Leland, Charles "Stormy" Mayo, Scott Marion, Scott Mercer, Judy Perkins, Mason Weinrich, and Hal Whitehead. Edith and Clinton Andrews, Brian Beck, W. Don Bowen, James R. Gilbert, Wyb Hoek, Bob Prescott, Arthur W. Mansfield, and Thomas G. Smith generously assisted us with new information about seals. Carleton Ray and Wes Tiffney, Jr., provided support for some of our seal research.

We thank Judith A. Beard for her great help over the years in organizing and maintaining most of the data gathered by the Gulf of Maine Whale Sighting Network, and we express our gratitude to the hundreds of people who have submitted accounts and photographs of marine mammals and other large sea creatures for our research files. That material has been valuable in the preparation of this book.

We thank all the people who contributed photographs for use in the present edition, and Lisa Carpenter, Michelle Frentrop, Stephen Mullane, and Jaki Waters for additional darkroom work. Be Sylvester gracefully turned outlandishly rough copy into typescript.

Although no grant or contract directly financed this book, we wish to acknowledge that it was started under a National Science Foundation Student Originated Studies grant to the College of the Atlantic (GY 11454) and that information or experience gained during projects funded by the Bureau of Land Management; the Carolyn Fund; the Massachusetts and National Audubon societies; the Marine Mammal Commission; the National Geographic Society; the National Marine Fisheries Service; and the World Wildlife Fund have all been important.

Despite all the help we have received, some mistakes will undoubtedly be found. We welcome any suggestions about how this guide could be made more accurate or useful.

Part One

WHALES, DOLPHINS, and PORPOISES

Introduction

THROUGH THE AGES, WHALES AND PEOPLE HAVE BEEN LINKED in myth, literature, art, music, and commerce. Until recently, people have tended to be interested mainly in products that could be made from whales, although some early scientists tried to learn about the whales themselves. As the apparently high intelligence and trainability of some porpoises (which are really small whales) became recognized during the past thirty years, public interest in the biology of whales increased. Recordings of the remarkable sounds of humpback whales, killer whales, and other marine mammals, as well as many recent films and articles, have stimulated public attention. Porpoises are popular exhibits at numerous seaquaria, allowing everyone a firsthand glimpse of their fascinating skills. Although a number of whales are already on the endangered species list, we know little about most of these creatures, whose unusual adaptations for life in the water make them some of the most interesting of mammals.

Humpback whale feeding on small fishes, with gannets diving for the leftovers. D. D. Tyler

3

All of the whales, dolphins, and porpoises belong to the order of mammals called cetaceans. Like the rest of the mammals, they breathe air with lungs, have warm blood, bear live young, and suckle them with milk from mammary glands. They differ from all other mammals in that they have no hind legs and no fur, except for a few hairs on the head in many species. The examination of living and fossil cetaceans suggests that they started evolving at least 45 or 50 million years ago from land mammals that had hind legs. However, many questions pertaining to their evolution remain unanswered. For example, we still do not know with certainty whether all living cetaceans share a similar distant ancestor. Furthermore, specialists disagree about whether cetaceans are descended from a cattlelike ancestor or from an animal more closely related to a primitive carnivore. The fact that the teeth of early fossil cetaceans bear some resemblance to carnivore teeth, and that all modern cetaceans have a strictly animal diet, favors the theory of a carnivore-like ancestor. On the other hand, modern cetaceans resemble ungulates (cattle and their relatives) in the structure of the stomach and in certain biochemical components.

We also do not know why cetaceans evolved, although reasonable speculation is possible. We may hypothesize, for example, that during the period of early cetacean evolution, much of the earth was covered by shallow seas. At certain places, such as along the coast of what is now North Africa, competition for food may have been intense on land. Some animals may have been able to find more food in the shallow water at the land's edge. After a while, competition may have reduced the abundance of easily available foods, favoring individuals that could swim better, feed in deeper water, or remain in the water longer. Natural selection has worked along these lines several times, starting with different ancestors, to produce the other marine mammals that we see today: the seals, sea otter, polar bear, manatees, and dugongs. In the case of the cetaceans, the tail evolved over the millennia into the major organ of locomotion. Wide flukes made of connective tissues and tendons developed on the sides of the tail for propulsion and steering. The cetacean tail beats up and down, rather than from side to side as in fish, mainly because the muscles used are basically the same as those used by the ancestral mammal for flexing the backbone up and down during running. Cetaceans, however, followed a completely different evolutionary path from that of their running ancestor, and they completely lost the hind limbs. All that remains of the legs is a pair of small bones that are vestiges of the pelvis, located near where the rear limbs of a land mammal would connect with the backbone. Meanwhile, the forelimbs evolved into relatively inflexible flippers, used mainly as stabilizers or for steering. Most cetaceans have a dorsal fin that helps to regulate body temperature and perhaps stabilizes the body during swimming.

The smooth, streamlined form of a whale or porpoise is created in large part by a thick layer of blubber, which makes up the innermost layer of skin. The blubber padding may be only an inch thick in dolphins or porpoises—which are usually less than 10 feet (3 m) long and weigh several hundred pounds—but it may be up to 2 feet (61 cm) thick in some of the larger whales, which may approach 100 feet (30 m) in length and 150 tons (136 metric tons). When a cetacean eats more than it requires for daily survival, the excess food is converted into fat and stored as blubber. If the cetacean eats less than its daily metabolism requires, fats are drawn from the blubber for immediate use. A cetacean must maintain a certain blubber thickness, not just for streamlining and food reserves, but also for thermal insulation. If the animal cannot catch enough prey, it will ultimately deplete its blubber thickness so much that it will be unable to maintain normal body temperature and will die. Finally, blubber helps to provide buoyancy, because it is lighter than water. A thin animal must work harder to stay afloat than a well-nourished one. Blubber was boiled down in times past to make oil for burning in lamps, for lubrication, and, more recently, for use in food products such as margarine.

The ancestors of whales must have breathed as land mammals do today, but the breathing mechanism has undergone considerable modification during cetacean evolution. The nostrils are located at the top of the head in nearly all living species, rather than at the snout tip as in other mammals. As a result, a whale can continue to swim as it breathes through this "blowhole," because only the very top of the head must break the water surface. In most large whales, the rostrom forward of the blowhole is raised as a splashguard to keep water from entering the nostrils. The specialized epiglottis separates the trachea and esophagus so effectively that whales and porpoises can breathe and swallow simultaneously. Cetaceans fill and empty their lungs much more quickly and completely than do other mammals, thus minimizing the amount of time spent at the surface. High concentrations of respiratory pigments in the blood and muscle bind large amounts of oxygen to maximize dive times. Whales and porpoises always inspire before diving, so people often wonder how they avoid "the bends." First, at depth the air is compressed to a very small volume. The ribs, which are usually not connected to the breastbone, are free to compress the lungs, forcing the air away from the absorptive lung surface and into bronchioles, bronchi, trachea, and— in toothed whales—airsacs near the blowhole. Second, lung compression reduces blood flow to the lungs, thus minimizing absorption of gases. Both processes, and perhaps others, prevent excessive quantities of nitrogen from dissolving in the blood. When a whale returns to the surface, its exhaled breath is often visible as a spout, probably caused by atomization of residual water from in or around the blowhole. In addition, the warm, moist, slightly compressed air from the lungs probably condenses when it encounters cold, saturated sea air. The sudden blast of exhaled breath can be heard for up to a half mile on a quiet day, and whales can often be located from a boat by stopping the engine in a favorable location and listening for blows. Small cetaceans do not always spout when they exhale and are therefore harder to spot at sea, but at close range their blows can also be heard.

The cetaceans are divided into two major suborders, the Odontoceti (from the Greek *odontos*, tooth, and *ketos*, whale) and the Mysticeti (Gr. *mystax*, mustache, referring to the hairy appearance of the baleen). Shown below are sketches of cetaceans from the two groups, which will familiarize readers with their shapes and the locations of external body parts.

Generalized Whale Types

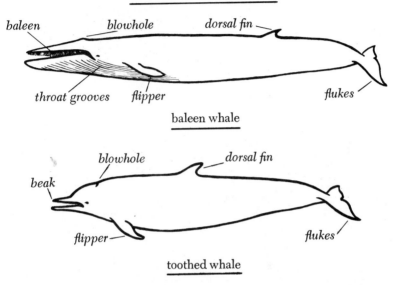

baleen whale

toothed whale

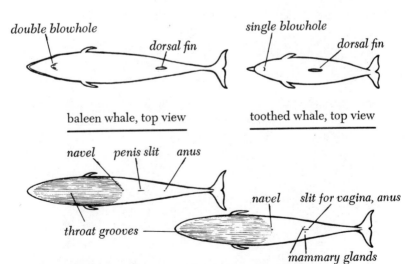

baleen whale, top view   toothed whale, top view

male and female baleen whales, seen from below

D. D. Tyler

Odontocetes, or toothed cetaceans, are usually well under 30 feet (9.1 m) in length. They generally pursue individual prey such as squid, fish, or—very rarely—birds or
mammals. Some species have been shown to use echolocation
to find food, and most other species are suspected of having
that ability. However, it is likely that porpoises, at least, can
locate food just by listening to sounds emitted by the prey.
Nearly eighty species of toothed cetaceans have been named,
and perhaps a few more will be discovered as we learn more
about the oceans. The smaller types are known as porpoises
or dolphins. People frequently ask which term is correct.
Technically, the dolphins and porpoises are classified in
separate families. The only consistent differences between
odontocetes in the families Delphinidae (Gr. *delphos,* dolphin) and Phocoenidae (Gr. *phokos,* seal, referring to the
seallike shape of the nominate species, the harbor porpoise)
is that delphinids have pointed teeth and phocoenids have
teeth that are flattened laterally. This difference cannot be
observed at sea. Adult delphinids are usually bigger (average 8–12 feet, or 2.4–3.7 m) than phocoenids (average about
5 feet, or 1.5 m). The delphinid snout is usually drawn out as
a beak, but phocoenids are blunt-snouted. Finally, although
both groups have members that lack a dorsal fin, delphinids
usually have large, curved fins and phocoenids usually have
small, triangular fins. In keeping with these differences, we
recommend the use of the name *dolphin* in reference to any
delphinid, and *porpoise* in reference to a phocoenid. Either
name can be used informally to refer to an unspecified small
odontocete, but the use of *porpoise* would eliminate possible
confusion with the widely distributed warm-water fish *Cory-
phaena hippurus,* whose common name is dolphin.

The skulls and "foreheads" of all odontocetes show, to
varying extents, anatomical modifications that are probably
associated with sound production and echolocation. In all
species, but especially in sperm whales (family Physeteri-
dae) and some of the beaked whales (family Ziphiidae), the
front of the skull has apparently evolved to be a sound re-
flector or wave guide for sound pulses. Similar, less dramatic
modifications can be seen in other species. The forehead in

most species contains a mass of oil-saturated tissue. Some species, such as the pilot or pothead whale (family Globicephalidae), have so much of this tissue that the front of the head bulges forward beyond the tip of the drawn-out jaws. The tissue is called the "melon" because it is rounded and has a firm, fibrous appearance when sliced open. The melons of some other species, such as the harbor porpoise, do not bulge past the jaws, but are still sufficiently large to obscure the beak, despite the fact that the skull of a phocoenid has jaws that are drawn out just like delphinid and all other odontocete jaws. The melon of delphinids is usually small enough so that the jaw protrusion can still be seen externally. Experiments suggest that the dense, oily melon tissue acts as an acoustic lens to focus sound pulses. The foreheads of sperm whales and some of the beaked whales have been modified even further to contain large quantities of a waxy liquid that may be used for buoyancy control and possibly for sound modification. Some observations and calculations suggest that odontocetes can produce sonar pulses intense enough to stun prey.

Mysticetes have no teeth, but instead possess a series of horny plates, called baleen or "whalebone," which hang down from the gum tissue of the upper jaw and whose frayed inner edges are used to filter food from the water. These whales are first seen as fossils from about 30 million years ago. Rudimentary tooth buds have been found in young embryos of some baleen whales, showing that the mysticetes are descended from toothed ancestors, but the fossil record provides little help in detailing the evolutionary steps. The mysticete whales in the genus *Balaenoptera* (the blue whale and its relatives) all have a number of folds or grooves on the throat and chest. When cut in cross-section, the ridge between each two grooves looks vaguely like a tube. Whalers named such whales "rorquals" from the Norwegian *ror*, tube, and *hval*, whale. The approximate maximum number of grooves in blue, finback, sei, and minke whales is, respectively, 88, 100, 56, and 70. In sei and minke whales the grooves do not extend much beyond the flippers, but in the other two species they reach the navel. The humpback whale has up to about twenty-five wide grooves that extend to the navel, so it, too, is a rorqual whale, although its morphology is different enough from those other species that it has been placed in a different genus. Rorqual whales usually feed by gulping single mouthfuls of water containing food. As water enters the mouth, the ventral grooves stretch, allowing the floor of the mouth to balloon outward so that the largest possible volume of water and food can be entrapped. The water is then squirted out through the baleen, leaving the food in the mouth and on the inner surfaces of the baleen. The tongue, which is much larger in baleen whales than in toothed species, must aid in squeezing out water and swallowing food, but the exact process has not been described.

Not all baleen whales are rorquals. The right whale and its relatives, the pygmy right whale and the bowhead (family Balaenidae), have no ventral grooves. Although they may filter single mouthfuls of water on occasion, they tend to filter feed continuously while swimming through shoals of small plankton animals such as copepods or krill. The gray whale (family Eschrichtidae), which is found only on the Pacific coast of North America but used to occur in the Atlantic also, has only two ventral grooves. Gray whales characteristically feed by scraping amphipods and other bottom organisms from the ocean floor at shallow depths.

Although some published evidence suggested the possibility that mysticete whales may produce sounds that could be used for echolocation, most researchers now doubt that active echolocation is important to these animals. Neverthe-

Baleen

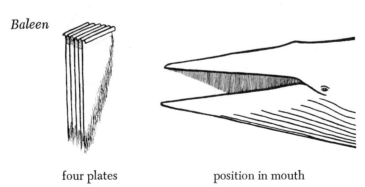

four plates   position in mouth

D. D. Tyler

Humpback whale snout, showing outside edges of approximately 125 baleen plates. Mason Weinrich

less, most mysticete species produce various sounds underwater and above water, whose significance is still being investigated.

In both the American and Canadian portion of our study area, whales have been important to people since aboriginal times and the earliest days of European settlement. As early as the 1500s, Basque whalers sailed all the way to the waters of Newfoundland looking for right whales, having hunted the species to near extinction along the European coast during the previous several hundred years. During subsequent centuries, occasional whales or porpoises were undoubtedly taken in eastern Canadian waters to supplement the predominantly fish diet of coastal residents. Whaling from shore stations took place at several locations in the Gulf of St. Lawrence during the 1800s. Large-scale hunting did not begin until 1947, when a fishery for minke whales opened at Dildo, Newfoundland, and began operations in Conception, Trinity, and Bonavista Bays. This was joined by a Nova Scotia fishery operating out of Blandford, which hunted minke whales from 1962 to 1964, then concentrated on finback and sei whales. Starting in 1951 the Dildo fishery also took pilot whales, and the catch of over 48,000 individuals during the subsequent decade caused the stock to decline sharply. All commercial whaling in Canada ceased in 1972. Coastal people still take meat from occasional whales or porpoises caught accidentally in shorefast nets or weirs, and a few porpoises are still hunted locally at times.

Coastal American Indians probably hunted porpoises and occasional right whales using canoes and spears, but no record of the hunt exists. English colonists who settled in Massachusetts were quick to notice the large number of whale spouts along that coast, promising them a good supply of meat and oil. Enlisting the aid of Indian harpooners, the settlers lost no time in starting to hunt right whales from shore stations around Cape Cod and adjoining waters, and they were successful in pursuing this fishery during the 1600s and early 1700s. Porpoises and pilot whales were also hunted or driven ashore during those years. As a result of this early whaling, by 1750 right whales were very rare along the U.S. coast, and they remain so today. During the nineteenth century, coastal whaling for humpback and finback whales was carried out along the Maine coast from ports such as Winter Harbor, Prospect Harbor, and Tremont. An average of six to seven whales, mostly finbacks, was taken annually from Prospect Harbor during 1835–40, the peak whaling years in that area. Large numbers of pilot whales continued to be driven ashore from Cape Cod Bay and Massachusetts Bay during the 1800s. Micmac Indians in the Bay of Fundy region hunted porpoises for oil in the late 1800s. Little hunting took place after 1900 in the Gulf of Maine. The migratory paths of most of our cetaceans are not clearly known, but it is possible that hunting in adjoining regions might affect the numbers of some species in our study area. At this time, the only one of our species that is still hunted commercially in the western North Atlantic Ocean is the minke whale, of which up to about 2,500 animals may be taken each year by Norwegian or Icelandic vessels in northern waters. The humpback whale is hunted along the coast of western Greenland (up to ten or twenty animals killed per year) and in the Grenadine Islands (perhaps one or two animals taken every year or two). Whether these losses affect the populations in our study area is not known.

Of more serious concern to cetacean populations in our area is the increasing frequency of fishery entanglements and entrapments. This problem has been most urgent in Canadian waters, where shore-fixed salmon and cod nets and, more recently, gill nets have been responsible for the deaths of many humpback whales, as well as other species. Such incidents have also occurred frequently enough in the Gulf of Maine to be of concern. In the Gulf of Maine, several minke whales get caught up in lobster fishing gear each sum-

Minke whale in fish weir, 1978. Dorsal fin and flank show signs of previous injury. Whale released unharmed. Steve Donosco

mer, and some minke whales, humpback whales, and porpoises become tangled in gill nets. Minke, humpback, and right whales, as well as other cetaceans, sometimes become trapped in herring weirs along the eastern Maine and New Brunswick coasts, but weir keepers are usually successful in freeing the animals unharmed. In all cases, loss of gear, fish, and fishing time may be a serious detriment to the fishermen.

Minke whale, head on. S. Harpswell, Maine, 1980. Whale drowned after entanglement in lobster fishing gear. Stomach contained seven mackerel. Steven Katona

Other threats to the well-being of cetacean populations include the increasing volume of shipping operations, with the attendant danger of collisions with whales and possible noise or disturbance to the animals; offshore oil production and oil spills resulting from tanker casualties; ocean pollution; and the preempting of important feeding or breeding areas by human activities. In most cases neither the magnitude of present effects nor of future threats is precisely known. Nevertheless, one cannot be overoptimistic about the long-term future of marine mammal populations if human domination of the ocean increases, regardless of whether the animals are hunted or not.

It was with these thoughts in mind that the first version of this field guide was prepared in 1975. Nothing stimulates concern for a species or habitat more than firsthand experience, and there was little question that an afternoon in the company of a whale or a quiet period of observation at a seal ledge would foster a lifetime of enthusiasm for the animals and concern for their welfare. Now, eight years later, New England has developed into one of the foremost areas for whale watching in the world, and Canada offers similar or greater potential. A combination of responsible self-restraint by boat owners and tour leaders with supervision by wardens entrusted with enforcing marine mammal and endangered species protective legislation is necessary to keep us from too much contact with the animals. We think those efforts have been successful in our study area, and that—for the most part—whale watching has thus far been to the long-term benefit of both whales and people. A list of whale-watching trips available in our study area will be found in Appendix II.

For those people fortunate enough to own a boat suitable for whale watching, additional possibilities exist. Fishing banks are excellent places to spot whales or porpoises, especially when schools of young fish are abundant. In the Gulf of Maine, Stellwagen Bank, Old and New Scantum's Ledges, and Jeffreys Ledge have been very productive sites for observing humpback, finback, and minke whales, and several species of porpoises. These banks appear to have whales earlier in the spring and later in the autumn than do the more northerly areas in the Gulf. From late June through early September, the waters around Matinicus Rock and nearby islands; Mt. Desert Rock; Cutler, Maine; outer Passamaquoddy Bay; Grand Manan Island, New Brunswick; and Brier Island, Nova Scotia, are often excellent sites for whales. It is unlikely that many yachtsmen will venture to Georges Bank or Browns Bank, but the Northeast Peak of Georges and the seaward edges of both banks are good places to see whales, and future years may see the development of whale-watching cruises to such locations. Our knowledge of good whale-watching areas along the coast of Nova Scotia is limited because there is less research and less boat traffic. Al-

Finback whale surfaces near whale watchers, showing white right lips. Scantums Ledge, Maine, October 21, 1981. Steven Katona

though we have received reports of memorable encounters with schools of pilot whales in several nearshore locations, most of the whales along the Nova Scotia coast appear to be farther offshore than is the case in other portions of our study area. Near the edge of the continental shelf offshore from Nova Scotia one is likely during the warmer months of the year to see finback, sei, and sperm whales along with a variety of dolphins. In addition, "the Gully," a deep, wide canyon in the shelf edge about 30 miles east of Sable Island, is one of the few places where the northern bottlenose whale has been seen with regularity. There are probably other still-undiscovered areas for good whale watching along the coast of Nova Scotia, and we welcome further information. The north shore of the Gulf of St. Lawrence offers the chance to see all the species mentioned above, plus occasional blue whales and belugas. Sites of particular interest include the confluence of the St. Lawrence and Saguenay rivers, the St.

Lawrence Channel, Sept Iles, the Mingan Islands, and Blanc Sablon. Much of Newfoundland's coast offers excellent whale-watching potential, as detailed further in the section on shore lookouts below. Finally, Newfoundland's Grand Bank is habitat for large numbers of whales during the summer, although it is beyond the reach of most readers. The Southeast Shoal of the Grand Bank appears to be used heavily by humpback whales during early summer.

Having mentioned some of the whale-watching possibilities open to boat owners, we feel obliged to offer some cautions. We strongly urge people to utilize commercial whale-watching tours whenever possible, rather than taking private boats to the same areas. Stellwagen Bank, for example, is so well served by commercial tours that there is no need to use a private boat. Minimizing the number of boats can only be beneficial to the whales. Private expeditions to less-traveled waters do not appear to pose a problem at this time, provided boat handlers exercise reasonable consideration for the whales. In particular, it is important to maintain a respectful distance (at least 50 yards, or 45 m) and to avoid any actions, such as gunning the motor, chasing whales, getting between a mother and her calf, or approaching sleeping, feeding, or courting whales, which cause the

Humpback whale lobtailing. Stellwagen Bank, summer 1980. Dotte Larsen

animals to alter their behavior and which could pose a danger to the whale or the boat.

Over the years we have received many letters or calls from boat owners asking whether they have any reason to fear the presence of whales. Sailing vessels making offshore passage at night or during heavy fog do face the small risk of hitting a whale. Whales sleep at the surface, and at such times they probably cannot hear an approaching sailboat. The probability of such a collision is low, judging from the few reports, and that is a comfort, since no preventive actions are available. Whales occasionally approach boats, inducing understandable fear in skippers and crew. Minke whales sometimes tag along with sailboats or swim under the hull of stopped vessels. Humpbacks have been reported to touch a boat. We have never heard of a case where an undisturbed whale approached and damaged a vessel in our waters. Killer whales are reported to have sunk several boats off the coast of South America in attacks that were unprovoked but may have involved accidental collisions. Such incidents are spectacular enough to attract attention, but they are so rare that they need not cause concern.

Finally, a class of incidents must be considered which involves provoked attacks or contributory actions by the boat. There are several documented accounts from the 1880s of sperm whales deliberately ramming and sinking whaling ships after being harpooned. While such an action seems understandable from the whale's point of view, so many whales have been harpooned during the past several hundred years that one ought to be impressed by their forbearance rather than by the few attacks they made on their persecutors. There have surely been numerous occasions on which observers, researchers, or divers approached whales too closely. In all cases of which we are aware, the whales have not harmed people or their boats, though on occasions they have given signals of annoyance or aggressive intention. We know of one instance in which a breaching humpback whale landed on a small boat that was drifting silently close by. Fortunately, there were no injuries, and the crew, all experienced whale watchers, thought that the whale simply didn't know the boat was there. The moral of that story is clear: small silent boats should not stay near large leaping whales. In another recent incident, a feeding humpback whale sank a boat near Portland, Maine, in 1981. Published recollections by that boat's owner leave little doubt that the boat was right in the middle of the whale's "bubble cloud." Humpbacks blow bubbles to concentrate prey, then rise through the middle of the bubble ring or cloud to eat them. Boats should never get close to a humpback's bubbles, or accidental collisions will occur. On the whole, we conclude that whales are much safer and more predictable than, for example, dogs. The alert, respectful seafarer has little to fear from their presence.

Some tips are in order for those readers of this guide who have never been to sea or seen a whale; who don't know what to look for; and who may very well wonder why all the other people on the whale-watching boat have jumped to the rail when there is apparently nothing to see. In fact, the first trace of a whale is usually a very small, far-off, undramatic puff of a spout that seems almost illusory as it vanishes in the wind. Perhaps fifteen seconds later it appears again, nearly a mile off. Now if you look closely in that direction, frustrated because you haven't seen it yet, you may just make out some specks in the sky. Those specks are sea birds, usually gannets, herring gulls, or terns, circling over the whales or porpoises, diving on the same fish school that the mammals are working. It may have been the birds that drew attention to the animals even before spouts were seen. Now that you know where to look, the next time the whale blows you will see your first spout. As the boat draws closer, you can make out a glistening black back, and perhaps a dorsal fin. You will suddenly find yourself both relieved, because you have finally seen a whale, and excited, because the boat is drawing up on the animal and the best is yet to come.

New whale watchers will find that only two things can spoil the fun, namely seasickness and cameras. Here are some ways to prevent seasickness. Eat a light breakfast, avoiding coffee, eggs, greasy food, and milk. Light tea and

Humpback whales surfacing near whale watchers and showing typical dorsal fin shapes. Jeffreys Ledge, October 21, 1981. Peter Stevick

lightly buttered toast are a safe bet. Dress warmly so that you can stay abovedeck in the fresh air. Do not take a seasick medication unless you have used that medication successfully before. In our experience, some of the pills make people feel worse. If you do decide to take medication, take it several hours before departure. Some people may want to explore alternative methods for control of seasickness. For example, capsules of powdered ginger root have recently been said to prevent motion sickness. Vitamin B complex may also be useful.

Do eat a light lunch aboard the boat. Follow one simple rule: eat only foods that will taste as good coming up as going down. We stick with apples, saltine crackers, and perhaps mild cheese sandwiches. If you do feel ill, either stand up in the fresh air and look at the horizon or, if necessary, lie down, preferably out of the way and abovedeck. Keep warm. Usually the sight of a whale brings remission to even desperate seasickness. If you do "lose your lunch" you will probably feel better immediately. Don't be ashamed of seasickness, for it is a common malady that afflicts nearly everyone at some time, including the present authors.

The reason cameras may tend to spoil your whale-watching fun is that you may be worried about the operation of your equipment; frustrated when you click the shutter too soon or too late; and either worried about whether your photographs will turn out well or, perhaps, disappointed that they didn't. Nevertheless, few people have the ability merely to experience the event without documenting it, so the following comments are in order. Check your equipment and film as soon as you get on the boat. Keep spray and whale breath off your lens with a plastic bag. Watch the whale for a while before you take any photos. Observe its rhythm and the timing of its behavior. Watch what other photographers are doing so you can learn from their successes and mistakes. Take a reflected light reading from a dark-colored object on the boat so that glare from the sea won't fool your camera. Double-check your shutter and lens settings with an experienced photographer. If the far-off whale looks like a dot in your viewfinder, it will look like a dot on your photo. In most cases the main ingredients in a good whale photograph are luck and the photographer's experience, so don't expect great photographs the first time you put to sea.

Whale watchers observing humpback whales flipper-slapping and rolling. Northwest Stellwagen Bank, September 3, 1982. Steven Katona

Fortunately for those who dislike being on boats, it is also possible to watch whales from shore at selected places along our coasts. In the Gulf of Maine, observations can be made during spring and summer from the dunes on Cape Cod, especially near Wellfleet, Truro, or Provincetown, where dolphins and occasional whales can be sighted starting in April or May. During the summer, harbor porpoises can often be seen from near the Bass Harbor Light and from other cliffs or headlands on Mt. Desert Island. July and August often bring good chances for seeing harbor porpoises, minke whales, finback whales, and occasional right whales or humpback whales from vantage points in the Passamaquoddy Bay region. The cliffs at West Quoddy Head State Park, near Lubec, Maine; Head Harbor Light on Campobello Island, New Brunswick, Canada; and the Swallowtail Light plus the cliffs at Northern Head and Southern Head on

Whale watchers and humpback whale inspecting each other. Northwest Stellwagen Bank, September 3, 1982. Steven Katona

Whale watchers get a close-up view of a humpback whale. North-west Stellwagen Bank, September 3, 1982. Steven Katona

Grand Manan Island, New Brunswick, all offer excellent lookouts.

Other lookouts are also present on the Canadian coast. Humpback and finback whales can sometimes be seen from Brier Island, the extreme southwest tip of Nova Scotia. We have not had many reports of shore sightings from other Nova Scotia sites and would welcome information about favorable locations. The cliffs at Cape Breton Highlands National Park, for example, would seem to have very good potential for whale watching. In Quebec, the lighthouse at Forillon National Park near the town of Gaspé and the cliffs near Les Escoumins and Tadoussac on the north shore of the Gulf of St. Lawrence can yield views of finback, minke, and —from the latter two stations—occasional blue whales. The Tadoussac site and the ferry dock at Rivière du Loup, directly across the St. Lawrence River, may provide sightings of beluga whales during late summer. Finally, Newfoundland's steep and forbidding coast can be a whale watcher's paradise, yielding sightings of humpback, finback, and minke whales plus pilot whales and several species of porpoises. All of the large bays will be home to whales during summer months, if inshore populations of the capelin on which they feed are abundant. Shore lookouts are possible at Placentia Bay (from near Cape St. Mary's Lighthouse); at Cape Race; at Conception Bay (cliffs near Bay de Verde); at Trinity Bay (town of Trinity); at Cape Bonavista (town of Elliston); at Bonavista Bay (town of Salvage); and at Fogo Island. Other sites will certainly be found along Newfoundland's extraordinary coast where cliffs overlook deep water.

Observers should keep in mind that not every trip to these places will yield sightings and that animals will usually be seen in the distance, visible perhaps only by their spouts. A 15× or 20× spotting telescope on a steady tripod is very useful at shore lookouts.

Species Accounts: Introduction

OUR STUDY AREA CONSTITUTES ONLY A SMALL PART OF THE known range of most of the species described below. Many of the species have populations in other oceans, and those populations may differ from ours in vital statistics such as size, reproductive rate, and even behavior. Whenever possible, the descriptions below feature information gathered from animals observed or sampled in our study area. We have noted instances where data from other locales have been used.

The twenty-two cetacean species described fall into four ecological groups, and it is largely these ecological differences between the species that account for their commonness or rarity in our study area.

GROUP I. Continental shelf, boreal. These species regularly occur on the continental shelf or near the coast in cool waters during at least part of the year, and are therefore frequently seen by whale watchers. They include finback, humpback, minke, and right whales; harbor porpoise, white-sided and white-beaked dolphins; killer whale and pilot whale.

GROUP II. Arctic or subarctic. The distribution of these species, although basically centered in very cold waters, extends south into our study area in specific places possessing favorable bottom topography, productivity, or other environmental factors. These species include the northern bottlenose whale, blue whale, and beluga.

GROUP III. Warm water or offshore. These species are common in the relatively warm, deep water at the edge of the continental shelf, over the continental slope, and farther offshore. They are only seen inshore in our area on rare occasions. These whales include the common, striped, and bottlenose dolphins; gray grampus, sperm whale, pygmy sperm whale; and perhaps the sei whale. Whales from the first two groups may also winter in this habitat.

GROUP IV. Rare warm-water beaked whales. The dense-beaked whale, True's beaked whale, and the North Sea beaked whale appear to be rare throughout their range, which is similar in extent to that described for Group III.

In the accounts that follow we discuss first the baleen whales, then the toothed whales. Within each group, the species are ordered by their apparent relative abundance within our study area. In most cases, each description of field marks begins with those characteristics visible at greatest distance. Features that are not visible at sea or not necessary for species identification are mentioned only briefly, if at all. A separate key for identification of dead or stranded specimens is included after the species accounts.

WHALES AND PORPOISES FOUND FROM CAPE COD TO NEWFOUNDLAND

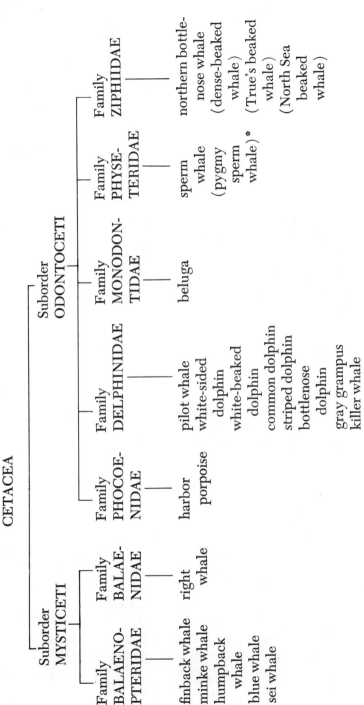

Order
CETACEA

Suborder
MYSTICETI

Suborder
ODONTOCETI

Family
BALAENO-
PTERIDAE

finback whale
minke whale
humpback
whale
blue whale
sei whale

Family
BALAE-
NIDAE

right
whale

Family
PHOCOE-
NIDAE

harbor
porpoise

Family
DELPHINIDAE

pilot whale
white-sided
dolphin
white-beaked
dolphin
common dolphin
striped dolphin
bottlenose
dolphin
gray grampus
killer whale

Family
MONODON-
TIDAE

beluga

Family
PHYSE-
TERIDAE

sperm
whale
(pygmy
sperm
whale) *

Family
ZIPHIIDAE

northern bottle-
nose whale
(dense-beaked
whale)
(True's beaked
whale)
(North Sea
beaked
whale)

* Note: Species in parentheses can be expected only as rare strandings.

Baleen Whales

FINBACK WHALE
(Balaenoptera physalus)

Finback Whale
size range: 30–70 feet
John R. Quinn

THIS SLEEK WHALE, SECOND IN SIZE ONLY TO THE BLUE WHALE, is found in all oceans and is the most common large baleen whale throughout our study area. In most places it will probably be the first big whale that a whale watcher sees, and it is often possible to judge a whale watcher's previous experience by his or her reaction to a finback. Quiet awe or an audible "Wow!" signify a novice. A blasé attitude, with sotto voce murmurings of impatience or disappointment, shows that the person has seen whales before and wants rarer or more acrobatic species. Finally, a person who remains quietly and carefully attentive is likely to be a seasoned whale watcher who realizes how little is known about the details of finback behavior, who wants to learn more firsthand, and who knows how interesting encounters with this species can be at times.

Finbacks are relatively easy to spot and tentatively identify at a distance because the robust spout, which rises up to 20 feet (6 m) on a windless day, and the prominent back and dorsal fin (up to 24 inches, or 60 cm) are easily seen. Finback whales often blow up to ten times at intervals of 15 or 20 seconds before diving for up to 10 minutes or more. The dorsal fin, whose shape and size varies among individuals, appears about 1 to 2 seconds after each blow. When starting a dive after a series of blows, a finback usually hunches up its back aft of the dorsal fin, but usually does not show its flukes. The scientific name of this whale (L. *balaena*, whale, + Gr. *pteron*, fin, and Gr. *phusa*, bellows) is not particularly descriptive aside from calling attention to the prominent dorsal fin and tall blow of the finback and its relatives.

Most people will require a closer look at the whale for confirmation of species identity. This may present a problem, because finbacks cannot always be approached. They are often restless or "spooky." They seem to avoid noisy boats, but sometimes come close to vessels dead in the water. They can be watched closely when feeding at the surface or on occasions when they lie quietly on a calm summer day. Then the distinctive asymmetric coloration of the head can be seen. On the right side of the head the lower lip, upper lip (usually), and anterior third of the baleen are white or pale gray. The lips and baleen of the left side are all dark. The white color of the right lip continues aft as a broad pale wash that sweeps up from the corner of the jaw to behind the

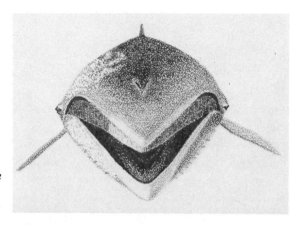

Finback Whale
front view
D. D. Tyler

blowhole. Two pale stripes called chevrons originate behind the blowhole and run aft, spreading to form a broad V along the back and upper side. The chevrons are best seen from above under good viewing conditions. The pale right lips, wash, and chevrons add fine and subtle variation to the otherwise dark back. While the coloration of the right lip and baleen is uniform among individuals, the color, intensity, and overall appearance of the chevrons and white wash can vary considerably among different animals. Some finbacks may lack chevrons altogether. Some individuals show pale orange or yellowish patches on the sides when seen up close in good light, perhaps as a result of overgrowth by diatom algae. If the whale rolls, you may be able to see that the white of the belly extends farther up on the right side than on the left.

The asymmetric head and body pigmentation is unique to finback whales, and may be important in their feeding behavior. Finbacks have a varied diet of fish, especially spawning and postspawning capelin, herring, and sand launce, probably supplemented by any of the other resources that may be abundant, notably krill and copepods. They feed at depth or at the surface, depending on where the prey is located. Descriptions of feeding are possible for shallow- or surface-feeding animals, but feeding methods at depth remain a mystery. Observations at the surface indicate that a finback frequently turns on its side when it opens its mouth.

Finback whale at autopsy, showing white baleen in front third of right jaw. This is the only whale in the world with this field mark. Brigantine Wildlife Refuge, N.J., April 15, 1975. Steven Katona

Individuals can be seen feeding with either side down. Side-swimming may allow the whale to turn more sharply. Finbacks have also been seen circling around or through a school of fish, often but not always in a clockwise direction. These observations have led to speculation that the white coloration of the right side of the head, and perhaps the lower right flank, could be used to startle fish and herd them into a confined area to make feeding easier if the whale swam in clockwise circles around its prey. However, it has also been suggested that the uneven head coloration may serve to camouflage the whale from the fish it pursues. Both

Finback whale, blowholes open. Shows splashguard, pale wash from right lips and right chevron. Jane M. Gibbs

tactics could be used in different situations, and many additional observations of feeding and perhaps other behavior will be necessary before the significance of the color pattern is fully understood.

Scientists from Woods Hole Oceanographic Institution are studying the acoustic behavior of the finback whale, which shares with the blue whale the distinction of possessing the deepest voice on earth. The typical call is about 20 Hz (cycles per second). The lowest note humans can hear is about 40 Hz. Loud single pulses may call other finbacks up to 25 km (15 miles) away. Repeated 20 Hz pulses about 8 to 12 seconds apart are made only in winter, apparently as part of courtship or reproductive display. Other slightly higher frequency sounds may be used for communication with nearby whales during feeding or diving.

North Atlantic finbacks are most abundant between New York and Labrador. Individuals can be seen anywhere from coastal waters to very deep waters, but the preferred feeding habitat is on the continental shelf in waters 50 to 100 fathoms deep. Some individuals apparently overwinter near Cape Cod, but in the Gulf of Maine the period of peak abundance is from about April through October. In the Gulf of St. Lawrence and in Newfoundland, finbacks occur from ice breakup in late March to freeze-up in November. In the Gulf of Maine, finbacks and humpbacks are often found together, but finbacks are usually found farther offshore in Newfoundland. When food is abundant, feeding groups of from several to perhaps forty finbacks can be seen.

Information from Canadian and other areas suggests that finbacks probably start to mate when about 5 or 6 years old and 57 to 60 feet (17.4–18.3 m) long, and females usually bear one calf every third year. The calf is 20 feet (6 m) long when it is born between December and April after nearly a year of pregnancy. The calf nurses for about 7 months before weaning, by which time it will be 36 feet (11 m) long. Young whales may feed on planktonic crustaceans such as copepods before assuming the adult diet, in which fish predominate. Finbacks can attain a maximum length of 79 feet (24 m). The potential longevity is not known.

Finback mother and calf, showing white right lips and chevrons. Mt. Desert Rock, Maine, August 1975. Steven Katona aerial photo

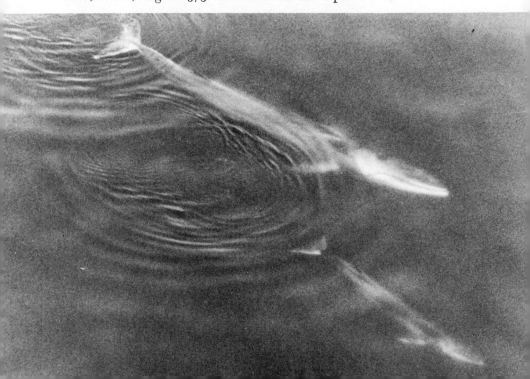

Finback whale feeding, right side down, showing baleen and distended mouth. New Scantums Ledge, Maine, May 17, 1980. Steven Katona

Finback whale. Mt. Desert Rock, Maine, summer 1980. Carol Haber

Several important questions need to be resolved for a satisfactory understanding of the ecology of this species in our study area, including the following: Where do the animals go in winter? Where does calving take place? How many separate stock units does the population include? And finally, how many finback whales are there in the various parts of the study area? The total population of finback whales in the whole North Atlantic before hunting took place has been estimated at between 30,000 and 50,000. In 1977 the International Whaling Commission's working group on North Atlantic whales gave an estimate of about 7,200 finback whales in Newfoundland and Nova Scotia. The University of Rhode Island's Cetacean and Turtle Assessment Program (CETAP) 1979 census estimate for U.S. continental shelf waters north of Cape Hatteras was a minimum of 1,100. The species seems much more numerous in eastern Canada, judging from kills of 4,000 (1903–15), 3,721 (1940–51), 3,248 (1945–51), and 2,386 (1966–72) in Newfoundland waters and 1,564 (1964–72) from Nova Scotia. A sustainable yield of perhaps 400 animals annually was considered

Finback whale. Mt. Desert Rock, Maine, summer 1981. Bob Bowman

possible in Newfoundland. It is not yet certain whether Newfoundland finbacks form a separate stock from finbacks that summer in Nova Scotia waters. An estimate of 569 finbacks offshore of southern Nova Scotia was made in 1971. The Gulf of St. Lawrence finback population, estimated at 340 animals in 1974, is supposed to be a separate stock unit. The current model, based on limited data, envisions the finback population broken into three or four feeding stocks that seasonally migrate relatively small distances offshore-onshore and north-south with very little overlap. Iceland and Norway are permitted by the International Whaling Commission to take up to 167 finbacks during 1982, but most or all hunting will take place east of our study area.

Finback whales showing variation in dorsal fins between individuals. Mt. Desert Rock, Maine, summer 1979. Bob Bowman

MINKE WHALE
(*Balaenoptera acutorostrata*)

Minke Whale
size range: 15–30 feet
John R. Quinn

The minke (pronounced "minky") is the smallest baleen whale in the study area. Its maximum length here is a bit over 28 feet (8.5 m). Younger animals range upward from 15 feet (4.6 m), so a second look may be required to make sure the whale is not a large porpoise. This species is seen fairly frequently, but is probably even more common than reports would indicate because it is more difficult to spot than the larger whales. This is because minke whales usually do not make a visible spout; they tend to avoid boats, but some individuals, especially young ones, may approach or follow stationary or moving vessels; they are often solitary; and they do not often breach (jump), lobtail (pound the water with the tail), or show flukes in our area. Breaching may be more common in some other parts of the minke's worldwide range. In general, most initial sightings of minke whales are happy accidents, when on a calm day the dorsal fin and back are seen out of the corner of the eye while the observer is looking at something else.

Behavioral field marks often must serve as species iden-

Minke Whale
top view
D. D. Tyler

tification for the minke because the distinctive morphological marking—a broad white band running across each flipper —can only be seen under the best conditions. The sharply pointed snout (the species name derives from L. *acutus,* sharp, pointed, + *rostrum,* snout, bill) characteristically breaks the water surface as the whale comes up for air. A typical breathing pattern might be two or three breaths at intervals of 30 seconds, followed by a dive of 2 or 3 minutes. The breathing pattern of an individual will often be very regular for an hour or more as it quietly goes about its business, ignoring or avoiding observers. On several occasions we have seen minke whales vanish completely and mysteriously after a long observation period at close range in a calm sea. We understood how such escapes are accomplished after watching one minke whale hold its breath for 17 minutes while it was being freed from a small fish weir. A minke could easily swim out of sight in that amount of time. The dorsal fin is quite prominent relative to the body size, and is usually strongly curved or hook-shaped, with its pointed tip directed backward. The fin and back are dark gray or black, but in good light a broad, whitish, crescent-shaped wash can be seen running up each side of the whale from behind the flipper toward the back. The pure porcelain-white belly and the short (up to 8 inches, or 20 cm), creamy-white baleen plates would usually be visible only on stranded minkes.

The overall range of this species in the western North Atlantic Ocean is from the subtropics to northern Labrador. The population apparently winters offshore and south to Puerto Rico and summers from Cape Cod north, but since

Minke whale showing pointed snout surfacing near a boat.
Dahl M. Duff

Minke whale dorsal fin. Cutler, Maine, August 1981. Steven
Katona

*Minke whale off Provincetown, Mass., April 18, 1976, showing dorsal fin
and white flipper patch.* Frank Gardner

Minke whale breaching in the Gulf of St. Lawrence, a lucky photo of behavior unusual for this species. J. Michael Williamson

no tagged individuals have been followed for very long, all speculations about migrations are based on the distribution of sighting reports. Minke whales are common at least from April through November in the Gulf of Maine and from March through November in the Gulf of St. Lawrence. Some are said to travel past Nova Scotia in May, and others reach Newfoundland in June or July and northern Labrador in August. Movements in Newfoundland are very strongly related to the capelin spawning migration. Minke whales may remain in Labrador until sea ice forms in November or December.

Mating is supposed to occur in winter or early spring, but it has never been observed. Males mature sexually when about 22 or 23 feet (6.7 or 7 m) long. Females mature when about 24 feet (7.3 m) long and 4 years old, then bear a 9-foot (2.8-m) calf each year or two, probably during October to March, after 10 to 11 months of pregnancy. Nursing lasts for less than 6 months. The maximum weight of a minke whale is about 11 tons (10 metric tons). A 21-foot (6.4-m) animal that we autopsied weighed 8,000 pounds (3,628 kg). No estimates of life span are available. Nearly all stranded individuals from the Gulf of Maine and farther south have been immature, whereas more northerly habitats have a higher percentage of mature specimens. Longevity is not known for minke whales in our study area, but the oldest individuals from the Southern Hemisphere appear to have been about 50 years of age.

Of all the baleen whales, the minke relies most exclusively on fish as food. Herring, capelin, cod, pollock, salmon, and mackerel are eaten, but some squid, krill, and even copepods are also taken. During summer, when schools of fish are inshore, minke whales can be found very near the coast in bays and shallow water. Data from the Newfoundland minke fishery suggests that juveniles and pregnant females come farther inshore than do adult males. Individuals sometimes become entangled in fishing gear.

Minke whale, showing white baleen and white flipper patch. Whale drowned after becoming entangled in lobster gear. S. Harpswell, Maine, September 1980. Steven Katona

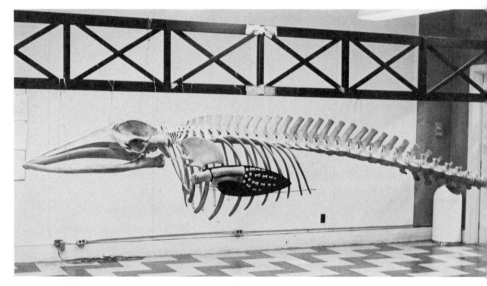

Skeleton of minke whale. Steven Katona

No reasonable estimate of the population of this whale in the western North Atlantic is available. Between 1955 and 1969 a total of about 530 minke whales was caught in Newfoundland waters. From 1978 through 1982 annual hunting quotas of about 2,500 minke whales have been in effect for the entire North Atlantic Ocean. Most of those animals are taken in the eastern North Atlantic by Norway or Iceland.

HUMPBACK WHALE
(Megaptera novaeangliae)

Humpback Whale
size range: 30–60 feet
John R. Quinn

The humpback whale, which is relatively common in the study area, has a marvelous set of field marks that make it perhaps the easiest baleen whale to identify in the field.

The first glimpse of a humpback might be the spout, which is about 10 feet (3 m) high and squatter and bushier than that of the finback. At times acrobatics, including breaching, lobtailing, spyhopping (poking the head out of the water), or waving the long white flippers, will attract attention. At close range any or all of the following features can be seen. The dark gray or black body, up to 60 feet (18 m) long, is somewhat stouter than that of the other rorqual whales. The head and snout bear knoblike swellings, each of which houses a stiff hair, which may help to detect prey or water currents. The dorsal fin is usually smaller than the fin-back's, more variably shaped, and often scarred or notched. The fin seems to be perched on a large hump. The name *humpback* may refer to the shape of the fin or to the series of small bumps, actually the tops of the neural spines of the caudal vertebrae, which appear on the back, aft of the fin, in some individuals. The whale takes its genus name (L. *mega*, big, + Gr. *pteron*, fin, wing) from the enormous white flippers, which are about one-third of the body length and may be used to maneuver, herd fish, guide calves, or pound the water for signaling position, showing aggression, or stunning fish. Waving the flippers in air may also help to cool the whale, which might be necessary at times in the subtropical waters of the humpback's breeding range.

jumping

Humpback Whale
D. D. Tyler

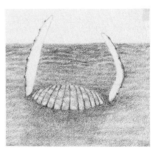

lying on its back at surface

The flukes are often raised nearly vertically out of the water when the whale dives, probably because this species descends at a steep angle. The trailing edges are irregular or sawtoothed. The ventral side of the flukes can be black, white, or any combination in between. Superimposed on the basic pattern are black or white scars from injuries or barnacles. Patterns are long-lasting, and individual whales can be recognized for many years from photographs of their flukes.

Humpback whale going down for a dive. Mt. Desert Rock, Maine, July 29, 1976. Steven Katona

The appearance of the dorsal fin and the pattern of black pigmentation near the base of the flippers are also individually distinctive. Collections of photographs are yielding excellent information on the migration, life histories, and population abundance of this species.

The rich behavioral repertoire of the humpback is still not completely described, but more than 15 years of work by scientists in the Atlantic and Pacific have produced significant insights. The wonderful songs (recorded on *Songs of the Humpback Whale* and *Deep Voices;* both Capitol Records) that first brought public attention to this species are now known to be produced only by males on the breeding range, apparently for the purpose of attracting females. During breeding, these "gentle giants" are not so gentle, and up to six or eight males cluster around a female or male-female pair, butting and jostling and lobtailing each other in competition for access to the female. These scuffles may produce some of the scars on the flukes, dorsal fins, or backs.

The humpback whale has populations in every ocean of

Humpback calf breaches. W. Quoddy Head, Maine, August 17, 1979.
Steven Savage

Humpback diving posture, showing lumpy dorsal fin and bumpy back.
Mt. Desert Rock, Maine, summer 1976. Ben Baxter

Right whale? Wrong! It's a humpback, whose bushy spout can resemble that of a right whale when seen from astern. Bermuda, April 1977. Bill Conrad (ORES)

Humpback whale spy-hopping. Wooden Ball Island, Maine, 1977. Ben Baxter

Humpback whale snout, showing sensory knobs, each bearing a coarse hair. Jeffreys Ledge, summer 1981. Jane M. Gibbs

Humpback whale lunge-feeding. Note water pouring from mouth and expanded floor of mouth. Mt. Desert Rock, Maine, July 1976. Ben Baxter

the world, but the first specimen formally described scientifically was obtained along the Maine coast, hence the species name, *novaeangliae,* from the Latin for New England. Western North Atlantic humpbacks now breed and calve principally in the warm shallow water of Silver, Navidad, and (less commonly) Mouchoir banks, north of the Dominican Republic, during January through March. Other locations in the West Indies or even near Bermuda might have been used in past times. After calving and/or mating, the whales migrate to feeding ranges in more productive northerly waters. The Gulf of Maine–Nova Scotia area, Newfoundland–Labrador, and Greenland all seem to harbor separate feeding populations, despite the fact that the animals appear to mix on the breeding grounds. A possible explanation for this separation is that whales follow the same migration route they learned as calves, when they followed their mothers north for the first time. Long-term migration information is now available for about 150 individuals.

Humpback whales, mouths wide open, feeding on sand launce offshore from Gloucester, Mass., summer 1982. Mason Weinrich

Examples of pattern variation in humpback whale flukes. Steven Katona

The breeding cycle of the humpback is also becoming better known. Whereas previous estimates suggested that females gave birth to a calf every 2 or 3 years, it is now known that some females in the Atlantic and in Hawaii produce a calf every year. Pregnancy lasts 11 to 12 months and the calf, 15 feet (4.5 m) long, nurses for up to a year, growing at the rate of up to 1.5 feet (45 cm) per month. The maternal instinct is very strong, and mothers do not abandon babies, even in extreme danger. Calves are about 25 to 28 feet (7.6–8.5 m) long at weaning. The age of first breeding is not yet precisely known.

Much new information has come to light on humpback feeding behavior. The diet is mainly schooling fish, including sand launce, herring, or capelin in different areas. Krill is eaten when abundant. Feeding methods appear to vary de-

pending on prey type, depth and abundance of prey concentrations, and local conditions. The different behaviors are used to concentrate prey before the whale gulps a single mouthful of water plus food, as do the other rorquals. Fish may sometimes be herded or stunned by lobtailing, flipper-slapping on the water surface, or flipper display under water. Several whales may together work a school of fish at depth or at the surface, each animal benefiting from limiting the directions of escape for the prey. Humpbacks have been seen to swim in a circle underneath a school of fish or krill while releasing a stream of bubbles. The rising bubbles form a temporary corral, which retains or concentrates the prey as the whale swims vertically upward with its mouth open. Boat operators must keep away from bubble clusters to avoid being struck by the whale when it surfaces. When food is abun-

Humpback whales, showing individually distinctive dorsal fins. Stellwagen Bank, 1981. Porter Turnbull

dant at the surface, humpbacks often lunge partway out of the water, jaws agape, water and fish streaming out of the mouth. Individual whales have been observed to patrol local areas in a regular feeding pattern for a week or more at a time. In the Gulf of Maine, finback whales and white-sided dolphins often feed along with humpback whales. White-beaked dolphins sometimes feed with humpbacks in the Gulf of St. Lawrence.

Since humpback whales are seen more easily from boats and airplanes than other species, and since they accumulate in local breeding sites, better population estimates are available for them than for other whales. Recent estimates of the total population of the western North Atlantic Ocean range between 2,000 and 4,000 animals, based on censuses carried out on the breeding banks. It seems likely from the collection of fluke photographs that the coastal waters of the Gulf of Maine contain at least several hundred whales; the Newfoundland–Labrador region contains up to several thousand whales; and the western Greenland coast contains at least several hundred whales. Humpbacks are relatively rare in the Gulf of St. Lawrence, but some are found along the north shore. The CETAP 1979 census survey produced an estimate of 684 humpbacks in U.S. shelf waters north of Cape Hatteras, but some of those animals could have been bound for Newfoundland. When fish schools are concentrated in summer or early autumn, it is not uncommon to see ten or twenty humpbacks within a few hours on Stellwagen Bank, off Cape Ann, or in the Jeffreys Ledge area of the Gulf of Maine. Larger numbers have been seen in the past and can be seen today during more extensive passages. Similarly, a Newfoundland bay may sometimes host hundreds of humpbacks, depending on capelin distribution, affording observers some truly spectacular whale watching.

Humpback whale, blowholes open. All baleen whales have a double blowhole. Steven Katona

Humpback whale flukes. Mt. Desert Rock, Maine, July 29, 1976. Steven Katona

Humpback whales have been fully protected by the International Whaling Commission since 1962 and no commercial hunting is allowed. Subsistence fisheries in the Grenadine Islands and along the west Greenland coast are permitted to take a total of about twelve whales per year.

RIGHT WHALE
(*Eubalaena glacialis*)

Right Whale
size range: 20–50 feet
John R. Quinn

The sighting of a right whale is one of the most exciting events in whale watching, both because the species is so rare and because it is so different from the other whales in our study area. The genus name, "true whale" (Gr. *eu*, good, + L. *balaena*, whale), reflects the fact that this was *the* whale in the early days of hunting. It was the "right" whale to hunt because it frequented the coast; swam slowly enough to be approached by sail or rowing; floated when killed (owing to the thick blubber layer); and yielded large amounts of oil and very long pieces of baleen. Centuries of hunting depleted the population, and what had once been a common species along the eastern American and Canadian coast became by the eighteenth century one of the region's rarest animals. Other populations of right whales, also depleted, occur in the South Atlantic, Pacific, and Indian oceans. This whale belongs to the family Balaenidae, which includes the bowhead, also known as the Greenland right whale, and the pygmy right whale, which occurs only in the Southern Hemisphere. The right whale's species name (L. *glacialis*, of

Right Whale

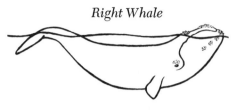

swimming at surface   D. D. Tyler

the ice) is somewhat inappropriate, because these animals appear to breed in temperate or subtropical waters even though they feed in boreal waters. The name *glacialis* would have been better used in reference to the bowhead whale, an arctic species that lives in close association with sea ice and that has never been reported with certainty on our coast south of Hudson Bay.

At a distance, the first clue to a right whale's identity is the low, bushy spout, which is V-shaped when seen from fore or aft, owing to the wide separation between the two blowholes. Right whales that we have observed have breathed from 5 to 10 times at intervals of 15 to 30 seconds before diving for from 5 to 15 minutes. When diving, right whales often show their flukes. The flukes are triangular, with pointed tips, smooth margins, and a deep central cleft.

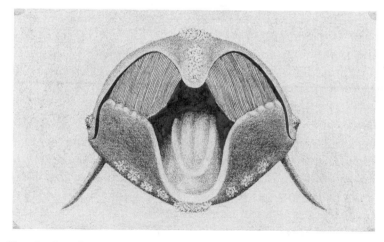

filter feeding, front view   D. D. Tyler

They are dark with occasional light scars. Even from a distance the complete absence of a dorsal fin can be noted, identifying the animal with near certainty as a right whale. Closer up, the fieldmarks are unmistakable. An adult right whale is between 35 and 50 feet (10.6–15 m) long. Its broad, fat back puts one in mind of a gargantuan hippopotamus. Body color is dark, often mottled with large patches of brown or light areas of sloughed skin. The huge head bears light-colored wartlike growths called "callosities" on the snout, around the blowholes, above the eyes, and along the lower jaws. The creamy or pink color of the callosities is due in large part to infestations of several species of cyamid amphipods, or whale lice. Callosity size, distribution, and number vary among individuals, and head photographs have been used to distinguish individuals over periods of years in Southern Hemisphere populations and recently in our own right whales.

Although right whales have occasionally been reported from the Gulf of St. Lawrence or Newfoundland during recent years, the place to see them most reliably is in the Gulf of Maine or off Nova Scotia. Right whales can be seen in Cape Cod Bay, Massachusetts Bay, on Stellwagen Bank, on Scantum's or Jeffreys Ledge, and off Cape Ann during April or early May. During July through September, they can be seen in outer Passamaquoddy Bay, off the Wolf Islands and Campobello Island, off Grand Manan Island, and on Browns Bank. In October and November, they can again be seen in ones or twos in the Scantum's Ledge area or off Cape Ann. The CETAP aerial surveys made numerous sightings of right whales on and inside of Georges Bank.

The Gulf of Maine appears to be important to right whales both as a feeding and a mating area. This species feeds primarily on planktonic crustaceans, especially the copepod (*Calanus finmarchicus*) and probably krill. Individuals select, by unknown means, areas of high plankton concentration, such as along windrows. Food is strained from the water continuously as the whale swims steadily through the plankton patch. Feeding in this manner is often called skimming.

Right whale, showing closed blowholes with callosities and broad, fat back. Offshore from Grand Manan Island, New Brunswick, August 19, 1981. Steven Katona

Right whale flukes, offshore from Grand Manan Island, New Brunswick, August 1982. Steven Katona

Right whales, offshore from Grand Manan Island, New Brunswick, August 19, 1981. Steven Katona

A whale weighing 50 tons (45.5 metric tons) or more could subsist on copepods (of which perhaps 4,000 would fit in a teaspoon) only if it had a large filtering apparatus. The massive head with its long arched jaw contains up to 390 plates of finely fringed dark gray baleen on each side. The longest plates are about 7 feet (2.1 m) in length. The baleen plates do not extend to the tip of the snout, and water can enter the mouth through the opening, about 1 square meter in a 50-foot (15-m) whale, between the left and right series of baleen plates, and can flow continuously through the baleen, leaving the plankton on the inside surface of the plates. There are no grooves on the throat of right whales or their relatives, probably because they do not take individual gulps of water while feeding. Right whales feed at depth or near the surface, depending on plankton abundance. Their preferred habitat appears to be on the continental shelf, and feeding has been seen in shallow water and in water up to 100 fathoms deep.

In recent years, right whale courtship behavior has been seen during August and September in water 80 to 100 fathoms deep offshore of Grand Manan Island, near Browns Bank, and also at Mt. Desert Rock, Maine. Pairs of animals

Right whale mother and calf in herring weir. Grand Manan Island, New Brunswick, August 2, 1976. Sydney Rathbun McKay

have been observed lying quietly together for hours at a time, occasionally touching each other with the head or flipper. Pairs, trios, or larger groups of up to six or seven whales sometimes roll or splash energetically, at which time the erect penis of a male can sometimes be seen. Researchers from the New England Aquarium are studying the details of this behavior. Mating had previously been reported to take place from April to July; pregnancy had been estimated to last about one year; and calves 13 to 18 feet (4–5.5 m) long were thought to be born from January to March. Some of those estimates could change as new information becomes available. The exact location of calving grounds is not known. Mother-calf pairs can be seen in spring in Cape Cod Bay and Massachusetts Bay and later in summer in the Passamaquoddy region. Females are very protective of calves. Juveniles may become sexually mature at 3 to 5 years of age. The average life span is not known, nor is the rate of reproduction for our study area.

During the colder period of the year from December through March, right whales are scarce in the Gulf of Maine, but sightings are reported from Florida, Bermuda, and the coasts of Georgia and the Carolinas. These observations plus historical data on the time and place of whaling kills suggest that the population performs annual migrations between those warmer waters and the northern feeding grounds. We do not yet know the migration routes of individuals or particular herds, or whether all individuals migrate. It is possible that some right whales bypass the inshore waters of the Gulf of Maine going to or from more northerly feeding areas. The feeding range used to encompass the Gulf of St. Lawrence, Newfoundland, and the Labrador coast, but centuries of hunting—beginning with Basque whalers in the 1400s—nearly extirpated right whales from those areas, and many decades may be required for repopulation.

Enlarged view of callosities of right whale, showing cyamid amphipods ("whale lice"). Steven Katona

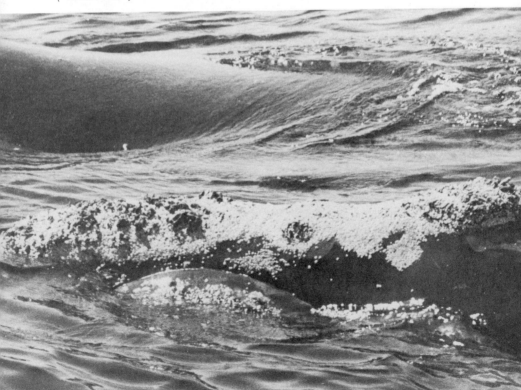

Right whale breaching, lower Bay of Fundy, summer 1982. Greg Stone

The number of right whales remaining in the western North Atlantic Ocean is not well known, but "guesstimates" have ranged from several dozen to several hundred. The highest single count, seventy, was obtained on April 13, 1970, in Cape Cod Bay by Woods Hole Oceanographic Institution scientists. CETAP aerial surveys in 1979 produced an estimate of at least twenty-nine animals in U.S. coastal waters (to the 100-fathom depth contour) from Cape Hatteras north. New England Aquarium workers have identified over fifty individuals in the outer Passamaquoddy Bay waters. During August 1980, one CETAP aerial survey counted forty-six right whales on Browns Bank. Right whales have been fully protected from hunting since 1937 by international treaty. Nevertheless, it still is unclear whether or not the population is increasing. The increasing numbers of sightings in recent years could be attributed to the growing numbers of whale watchers and more research effort, or they could be the result of the changing distribution of animals, perhaps in response to human disturbance or competition from other whale species. We feel that recent sightings justify some optimism that a slow recovery of the population may be occurring, but in any case one must wonder why the species has not made more progress during forty-five years of protection.

BLUE WHALE
(Balaenoptera musculus)

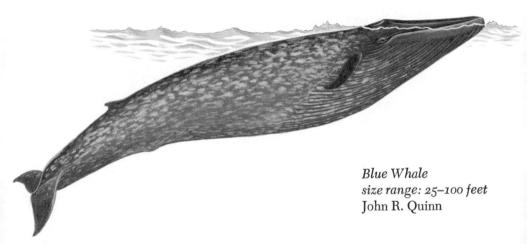

Blue Whale
size range: 25–100 feet
John R. Quinn

In the previous editions of this guide (1975 and 1977) we elected to include the blue whale because we suspected that occasional individuals might be found around the outer banks fringing the Gulf of Maine, even though no reliable sightings had ever been reported within this area. In August 1980, the CETAP aerial survey observed two blue whales on Browns Bank, and an experienced whale watcher saw another near Georges Bank on June 15, 1982. A very large, white-spotted whale observed at the end of July 1981 on Jeffreys Ledge was originally suspected to be a blue whale, but probably was not. However, expansion of the study area to include eastern Canadian waters requires consideration of the species, because blue whales can be seen regularly during summer in the Gulf of St. Lawrence, and others may be found in the Strait of Belle Isle, around southern and northeastern Newfoundland, and on the Grand Bank.

At a distance, a blue whale would look like a very big finback whale, showing a very tall, straight spout of up to 20 feet (6 m) or more in still air, a long, dark back, and a small dorsal fin. Observers familiar with the appearance of finback whales would notice the following differences: (1) the spout is taller and stronger; (2) since the whale is so long (adults to 85 feet [26 m] or more in our area) and the dorsal fin is situated so far aft, much more time elapses (up to 3 or 4 seconds) between the spout and the appearance of the dorsal fin; (3) the dorsal fin, less than 1 foot (25 cm) high, is smaller, both absolutely and relative to the huge body; (4) the flukes often clear the water briefly as the whale dives. Drawing closer, suspicions aroused, one would need to note the following characteristics. The blue-gray color of the sides and back is mottled with irregular light spots. The blowholes are shielded by a conspicuously raised splashguard that continues forward as a short rostral ridge. The rostral ridge is usually noticeably shorter than the finback's, and the rostrum is broader and more rounded, rather like an old-fashioned ironing board. Also in contrast to the finback, both sides of the head are dark, and chevrons are less conspicuous or absent.

Blue whale, showing rounded rostrum with short rostral ridge, large rostral splashguard, and mottling on back. Gulf of St. Lawrence, 1981. Richard Sears

Blue whale, showing huge size, mottling, and small dorsal fin. Mingan Islands, Gulf of St. Lawrence. Richard Sears

If the animal you spotted was really a blue whale, you would undoubtedly be impressed by its size, for this is the largest animal alive today and probably the largest that has ever lived on this planet. The record for size was set by an Antarctic female 106 feet (32.3 m) long which is supposed to have weighed over 150 tons (136 metric tons), but bigger individuals may have existed. As is true in all the baleen whale species, Northern Hemisphere individuals are somewhat smaller than those from the Southern Hemisphere. Adults grow to about 85 feet (26 m) in Newfoundland waters, averaging about 70 feet (21 m). There can be little doubt that Linnaeus, who was fluent in Latin, had tongue in cheek when he assigned the blue whale its specific name, because *musculus* means muscle but also can be translated as "little mouse."

The distribution of blue whales in summer is determined largely by the abundance of krill, their exclusive food. Krill

Blue whale, showing distinctive dorsal fin shape and typical skin mottling. Mingan Islands, Gulf of St. Lawrence. Richard Sears

concentrations dense enough to support a blue whale are found in places where deep water rich in nutrients upwells to the surface, nourishing heavy blooms of phytoplankton and a productive planktonic food chain. The outflow of the mighty St. Lawrence River, which equals the total flow of all the rivers on the U.S. East Coast, provides nutrients and also helps to create upwelling along the north shore of the Gulf of St. Lawrence as deep water replaces the outflowing surface layer. Here and in other productive spots, a medium-sized blue whale weighing 100 tons (91 metric tons) would eat up to 4 tons (3.6 metric tons) of krill each day during the feeding season, gulp-feeding, then straining water out through the 3-foot (91-cm), dark, coarse-bristled baleen. Scientists at the Mingan Islands Cetacean Project in the Gulf of St. Lawrence have observed blue whales feeding on their sides, ventral grooves ballooned out to enclose tremendous mouthfuls of 50 to 70 tons of water plus krill.

Little is known about the reproduction of blue whales from our region. In the Southern Hemisphere, baby blue whales are about 23 to 27 feet (7–8.2 m) long and weigh 3 to 4 tons (2.7–3.6 metric tons). They gain up to 200 pounds (90 kg) per day during nursing, which lasts about 7 or 8 months. Females give birth every 2 or 3 years, following gestation of about a year. Potential longevity is probably comparable to a human lifetime, but few data are available. No information is available on the winter range of western North Atlantic blue whales, but it is supposed that they migrate offshore and perhaps south, to warmer oceanic waters. Mating and calving are thought to take place somewhere on the winter range.

During recent years, fears have often been expressed that blue whales might become extinct as a result of excessive hunting. The latest estimate suggests that perhaps 15,000 blue whales still exist throughout the Atlantic, Pacific, Indian, and Antarctic oceans. Whether this number is correct or not, it is important to remember that over twice that many blue whales were killed in the 1930–31 Antarctic whaling season alone, and it is a great tragedy that this species has been so severely reduced from an estimated worldwide prewhaling population of perhaps 300,000 individuals. The hunting of blue whales has been prohibited in all regions since 1967 by the International Whaling Commission, and although some outlaw hunting may still occur, the population ought to begin a slow recovery. Several centuries may be necessary to see whether the blue whale will, in fact, escape extinction.

Few data are available on the number of blue whales in the western North Atlantic. Between 1898 and 1915, Newfoundland and Quebec whalers killed a total of about 1,500 blue whales, mainly during June and July, off the south and west coasts of Newfoundland and in the northern Gulf of St. Lawrence. Rough estimates of the prewhaling population, based largely on those data, range from 1,100 to 1,500. A 1981 census flight located at least fifty blue whales in the northern Gulf of St. Lawrence, where efforts are under way to identify individuals by natural markings. Although CETAP did identify two blue whales off the coast of Nova Scotia in 1980, their 1979, 1980, and 1981 census flights found no blue whales in U.S. shelf waters north of Cape Hatteras and out to 100 fathoms.

Blue whale flukes, showing some scars that can be used for individual identification. Mingan Islands, Gulf of St. Lawrence. Richard Sears

SEI WHALE
(Balaenoptera borealis)

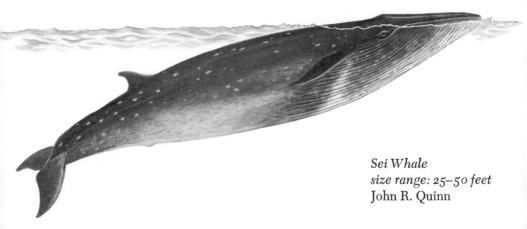

Sei Whale
size range: 25–50 feet
John R. Quinn

Sei (pronounced "say") whales are found throughout the world ocean, and in the western North Atlantic they are known from Davis Strait to Venezuela and the Gulf of Mexico. They are infrequently seen in U.S. waters, but are somewhat more common off Nova Scotia and farther east. Few amateur whale watchers have ever seen and identified this species, and probably only experienced whale hunters could at a distance reliably discriminate the shorter, less dense blow of a sei whale from that of a finback whale or separate the species by profiles or behavior. Anyone else would be well cautioned to get a good close look and make certain of the following characteristics before crying "Sei!"

The sei is smaller than the finback, rarely exceeding 50 feet (15 m). Its head is uniformly dark on both sides, in contrast to the asymmetric coloration of the finback's head. The body is dark above, lighter below. In Antarctic and Pacific sei whales the dark skin of the sides is dotted with many light oblong spots, each about 4 inches (10 cm) long by 1 inch (2.5 cm) wide, caused by a parasitic copepod. In comparison, finback flanks are rarely spotted, and the light mottling of the skin of a blue whale does not usually give the "spotted" appearance attributed to sei whales. Sei whales in the Atlantic Ocean do not have dramatically spotted sides, but instead appear to be uniformly darker in color than finbacks.

Whalers used to identify sei whales mainly by their swimming behavior, which tended to be faster and with more erratic changes of direction than was the case for the other rorqual whales. Aerial observations by scientists from Woods Hole Oceanographic Institution of one of the few sei whales definitely identified in the Gulf of Maine revealed that same type of swimming during feeding. A sei whale may show its snout when it surfaces to breathe, but it usually shows little of itself above water and does not arch the back when diving. The dorsal fin, which appears simultaneously with the blow, is usually relatively taller, thinner, and more deeply hooked in the sei whale than in the finback, and it is also placed farther forward on the back. However, fin shape certainly intergrades between the species. Readers are cautioned that many of the existing descriptions of sei whale

Dorsal fin of sei whale seen off Ocean City, Maryland. Fin shape alone should not be used to identify rorqual whales. Peggy Edds

swimming behavior were made of whales being pursued by whaling ships or at least in areas where whale hunting was occurring. Undisturbed animals could behave somewhat differently.

Unlike other rorqual whales, sei whales often skim feed as right whales do, continuously filtering small planktonic crustaceans such as copepods (*Calanus* spp.) and several species of krill. The black baleen has a very fine silky fringe of white bristles that allow the whale to filter those small animals. Over 75 percent of the sei whales killed off Nova Scotia in summer had copepods in their stomachs. Sei whales have been seen swimming slowly just below the surface, with mouths slightly open, presumably skimming plankton, covering several hundred feet between breaths, but not selecting the richest plankton patches as right whales do. At such times the breathing can be slow and regular, with a single breath followed by several minutes of feeding. A sei whale spouting in this manner might be harder to notice than a whale that spouts several times in succession. However, sei whales can also dive for food or pursue fish, and the existence of ventral grooves on the floor of the mouth suggests that obtaining large gulps of water plus food must be an important method of feeding. Gulp-feeding must predominate in portions of our study area because the stomachs of sei whales killed in Newfoundland contained capelin and krill, but no copepods. When feeding at depth the sei whale's breathing rhythm might be similar to that of other baleen whales.

Post-mortem examination of about 400 sei whales caught by the Blandford, Nova Scotia, whaling station from 1967 to 1970 showed that sei whales mate in January and February after they have attained lengths of 40 to 45 feet (12–14 m). Pregnancy lasts 10 to 12 months, and females may bear a calf every 2 or 3 years. The 15-foot (4.5-m) calf nurses for about 7 months, growing at the rate of nearly 1 inch (2.5 cm) in length per day. The longevity of a sei whale is supposed to be up to 70 years.

Relatively little is known about the number of sei whales in our study area. The 1979 CETAP survey effort (over

Sei whale on cutting deck at Blandford, Nova Scotia, September 1970. Note that right side of head is dark, as is the baleen, and that the flank is not noticeably spotted. Everett Boutilier

16,000 hours of on-watch observation) located only five definitely identified sei whales in U.S. shelf waters north of Cape Hatteras, all in late spring to summer on the edge of the continental shelf southeast of Georges Bank. In 1980, CETAP personnel saw forty sei whales feeding near finback and humpback whales along the continental shelf break at Hydrographer's Canyon, slightly south of our study area. Canadian census data obtained in 1969 suggests that Newfoundland–Labrador (at least 965 whales) and Nova Scotia (over 870 whales) harbored separate population stocks. The total western North Atlantic population was estimated to be 2,078 whales in 1977.

Much of the difficulty in locating or counting sei whales may be a result of unknown factors in the ecology of the species. In northern European waters the seasonal appearance of sei whales has frequently been described as unpredictable. It is from descriptions in those waters that the whale takes both its species name (L. *borealis*, northern) and its common name. *Seje* is the Norwegian name for pollock, and sei whales tended to appear off the Norwegian coast at the time when pollock were first caught, but the number of whales seen in different years varied widely. Peak catches off Nova Scotia occurred in June–July and late August–September, suggesting that many whales moved past Nova Scotia in early summer, then returned in late summer. Sei whales were taken off northeastern Newfoundland and Labrador only in August and September. If the factors governing sei whale habitat choice and migration were better understood, one would have a better idea of where and when to look for these animals.

Toothed Whales

HARBOR PORPOISE
(Phocoena phocoena)

Harbor Porpoise
size range: 4–6 feet
John R. Quinn

THIS LITTLE PORPOISE IS FOUND FROM CAPE HATTERAS TO
Greenland but is most abundant in the Gulf of Maine and off
Nova Scotia, where it is the most commonly seen cetacean.
It is moderately common in the Gulf of St. Lawrence, but

Harbor porpoise, showing triangular dorsal fin. Steven Katona

less frequently seen in Newfoundland. Populations of harbor porpoises also occur in cool waters in Europe and along the U.S. West Coast. This is one of the smallest cetaceans, reaching only 5 feet (1.5 m) and about 140 pounds (64 kg). Its small size and undemonstrative nature make it difficult to observe in any kind of sea. However, on a calm day from about April through October, anyone sailing along our coast and keeping a sharp lookout will surely see this species.

Observers must rely on relatively few characteristics for identification. Most easily seen and most definitive is the triangular dorsal fin with its sloped, slightly curved trailing edge. It is unlike the fin of any other small cetacean in the study area. Closer up, a wash of pale gray can be seen running up the flanks forward of the dorsal fin, gradually blending into the dark gray of the rest of the body. The absence of an external beak can be noted during very fast swimming, when harbor porpoises tend to breast the surface. Under most conditions harbor porpoises ignore or avoid boats underway. However, they sometimes approach a stopped boat. The best way to observe harbor porpoises is to drift among them in a small boat on an absolutely calm, sunny day. The porpoises will sometimes come close to the boat, and as they swim around and under it you will be able to see clearly the field marks discussed above, some of the more subtle markings that can be individually distinctive, and also the powerful up and down beat of the flukes. When the sea is calm, harbor porpoises can also be seen basking motionless at the surface.

During early spring in Gulf of Maine waters, harbor porpoises appear individually or in small, loose groups, but from August through September larger groups of twenty or more porpoises are sometimes seen. Groups of up to one or two hundred animals are seen in the Gulf of St. Lawrence from about May to November. No one knows where harbor porpoises go in winter, but most individuals desert inshore waters.

Harbor porpoises do not make a visible spout, but the soft puffing sound of exhalation can be heard for perhaps a hun-

Harbor porpoise near Mt. Desert Island, Maine, summer 1978, showing no beak and light thorax patch. Scott Kraus

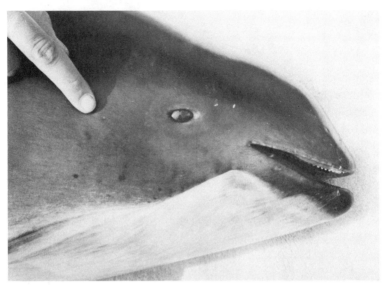
Harbor porpoise head. Finger indicates external ear opening.
Steven Katona

dred yards on a quiet day, giving the animal its local name,
"puffer" or "puffing pig." The term *porpoise* derives from the
Latin *porcus*, pig, plus *piscus*, fish. The specific name simply
comes from the Greek *phokaina*, meaning porpoise. A harbor
porpoise typically breathes three to four times, with intervals
of a few to 30 seconds between breaths, then dives for 3 to
4 minutes.

Probably the small size and short dive times of harbor
porpoises are related to their habitat requirements. They are
nearly always found in relatively shallow water on the continental shelf. In summer, harbor porpoises often come very
close to shore and even into harbors or tidal rivers in pursuit
of herring (Maine fishermen often call them "herring hogs"),
mackerel, capelin, hake, pollock, and squid. Even when harbor porpoises are found far from shore, they will be on shoal
banks, such as Georges Bank. In shallow waters, the harbor
porpoise consumes a relatively diverse diet of bottom-living
fishes and invertebrates, in addition to the schooling fishes
that are its staple. Each harbor porpoise will eat about thirty-
five to forty times its body weight in food each year.

The facts that harbor porpoises come close to shore and
are manageably small, and that specimens can be captured
or obtained from accidental entanglements in fishery gear,
have helped scientists to learn much about their physiology,

anatomy, and ecology. Young are born from April through July, after 11 months of pregnancy. Sexual maturity is reached at ages 4 to 6, and females probably bear a calf each year. This is one of the shortest-lived of all cetaceans, with a maximum longevity of about 13 years. Despite their undemonstrative nature in the wild, harbor porpoises have been highly trainable at several aquaria in the United States and Europe.

No census estimates for the entire study area or for Canadian waters are available. The northern portion of the Gulf of Maine appears to contain the bulk of the U.S. population of this species. A minimum of 4,000 harbor porpoises are estimated to inhabit the waters of Passamaquoddy Bay and the approaches to the Bay of Fundy. The inshore habitat of the harbor porpoise makes it especially vulnerable to environmental pollution, entanglement in gill nets, and possibly human disturbance, but the response of the population is not yet known. Those factors appear to be much more threatening to the Fundy region population than the small subsistence hunting take by Passamaquoddy Indians near Eastport, Maine. No population estimates are available for harbor porpoises in other parts of the study area.

Harbor porpoise head, showing flattened teeth characteristic of family Phocoenidae. Steven Katona

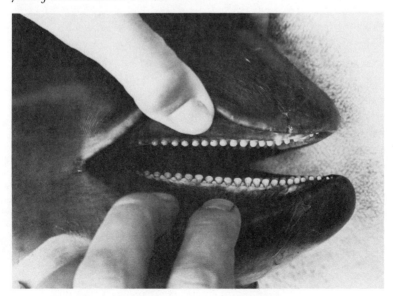

PILOT WHALE
(Globicephala melaena)

Pilot Whale
size range: 10–20 feet
John R. Quinn

The key to the distribution of these medium-sized whales, which reach a length of 20 feet (6 m) and a weight of 3 tons (2.7 metric tons) and average 13 feet (4 m) and about 1,800 pounds (816 kg), is the location of schools of squid, their exclusive food. Fish, especially cod, are eaten only if no squid are available. Vessels at the edge of the continental shelf, where water depths quickly descend from 100 fathoms to the ocean floor, and where squid are abundant, will encounter schools of pilot whales throughout the year. The common squid in our study area, *Illex illecebrosus*, migrates over the shelf toward inshore waters during summer and early autumn for feeding on herring, mackerel, and capelin. Large schools of pilot whales follow the squid into Newfoundland waters and, to a somewhat lesser degree, into the Gulf of St. Lawrence, Nova Scotian waters, and the Gulf of Maine. During each year a pilot whale will eat between fifteen and eighteen times its body weight in squid, and the 50 tons (45 metric tons) or so that a big male annually requires might include nearly 250,000 squid.

Pilot whales are relatively easy to identify. They are entirely jet black (hence their species name, *melaena*, from Gr. *melas*, black, and their local name, "blackfish"), except for a light-colored, anchor-shaped patch on the belly, which is only rarely visible at sea. The dorsal fin is unmistakable in shape. It is large, very long at the base, strongly curved, and rounded at the tip. Sexual dimorphism in fin shape occurs. Males develop longer-based, blunter-tipped fins with thickened leading edges. The total body length of males also averages about 20 percent greater than that of females. The head is very bulbous, owing to the large rounded melon, giving the whale its common name "pothead" and its species name (L. *globus*, ball, + Gr. *kephale*, head). In old animals the melon can protrude beyond the snout. Pilot whales can be seen singly or in schools up to several hundred or more, but the average school size is about twenty. Lobtailing, spyhopping, and basking at the surface are frequently seen behaviors, but bowriding and breaching are not common. For unknown reasons pilot whales and bottlenose dolphins (*Tursiops truncatus*) are often seen together offshore. They have also been seen mingling with right whales on Browns Bank and near Mt. Desert Rock. White-sided dolphins school with them on occasion in Newfoundland.

This species is known from both sides of the North Atlantic Ocean, and a nearly identical form exists in the South Atlantic Ocean. In the western North Atlantic it ranges from North Carolina to Greenland. Another very closely related species, the short-finned pilot whale (*G. machrorynchus*), extends from about New York south. The two species are indistinguishable at sea, but the rather diffuse boundary is far enough south of our study area that animals seen north of Cape Cod are almost certainly *G. melaena*.

Throughout their range pilot whales have been hunted for meat and oil. In the Gulf of Maine, where their presence and abundance are apparently quite variable from year to year, thousands of pilot whales were driven ashore in Massachusetts from the 1700s to the 1920s. For example, a herd of 2,300 was killed in 1874, a year in which at least

This pilot whale was unexpectedly taken by rod and reel from a sportfishing boat out of Round Pond, Maine, on August 28, 1966. Everett Boutilier

3,000 animals were caught. Excessive hunting in Newfoundland waters, where 47,078 potheads were taken from 1951 to 1961, is believed to have lowered the population markedly from an estimated prewhaling population of 50,000–60,000 animals. The standard method for hunting pilot whales is to surround a school near shore with several boats, then drive the animals toward the coast by making as much noise and commotion as possible. The gregarious nature of the individuals works to their disadvantage as they cluster closer and closer until there is no escape. This hunting technique, which is still used today in some places, was probably also employed by the aboriginal inhabitants of our coasts. The social behavior of the pilot whales is mediated by their underwater calls, a complex repertoire of species-specific but individually distinctive whistles. It is possible that each school has one or more leaders and that whales will not stray from the leader— even in a precarious situation—as long as it emits calls of distress.

The same characteristics that allow pilot whale schools to be herded are probably also a factor in the frequency with which schools strand themselves on shore. Additional contributing factors might include difficulty in detecting a gradually sloping bottom; extraordinary tidal amplitude in some locations; inattention to depth or bottom topography during frenzied feeding; stormy weather with strong on-shore wind or tide; parasite infestation of the inner ear; and leader error. Since the species is basically pelagic in deep water, schools and their leaders probably do not have much experience negotiating nearshore waters. Whatever the contributing factors, once the leader or perhaps other school members begin to emit distress calls, the remaining

Some of the approximately forty pilot whales that swam into Castine Harbor, Maine, on July 29, 1981. The whales were successfully driven out. Arthur B. Layton, Jr.

Pilot whales offshore from Mt. Desert Island, Maine, September 9, 1982.
Scott Marion

animals apparently refuse to leave them. This phenomenon is probably responsible for the tragic determination of school members to come ashore time and again, to the puzzlement and dismay of people trying to rescue them. As is the case with most cetacean mass strandings, once pilot whales initially beach themselves, efforts to return them to the water merely result in the animals' restranding themselves over and over again. It is possible that the most effective way to prevent mass death when a school begins to strand might be to isolate or shoot beached animals immediately so that they do not draw other school members ashore with their distress cries.

The reproductive cycle of pilot whales is reasonably well known. Females mature sexually at about age 6 and males at age 12 or 13. In Newfoundland animals, pregnancy lasts about 16 months, and the calf, 5.5 feet (1.7 m) long at birth, nurses for about 20 months. A female will probably give birth to five or six calves during her lifetime. The maximum life span is estimated at twenty-five years.

WHITE-SIDED DOLPHIN
(Lagenorhynchus acutus)

White-sided Dolphin
size range: 7–9 feet
John R. Quinn

This lovely, energetic dolphin is common throughout the study area. It ranges in size from about 6.5 to 9 feet (1.9–2.8 m), which is close enough to the size of other local dolphin species to make identification by size impossible. It is always necessary to get a good look at the color pattern on a dolphin's sides in order to identify it. The field marks are distinctive enough on the dolphins in our area so that observers will have no difficulty in separating the species.

The distinguishing mark in this species is the sharply defined narrow white patch on the side which begins below the dorsal fin and runs aft. Several feet back, the white patch terminates abruptly, to be continued by an equally sharply defined patch of yellow or tan. The yellowish patch runs up toward, but not over, the dorsal ridge of the tail. One can also note that the short beak, back, sharply pointed dorsal fin (the species name comes from L. *acutus*, sharp, and refers to the dorsal fin), and flippers are all black; the flank is a lighter gray; and the belly is white.

White-sided dolphin breaching near Mt. Desert Rock, Maine, August 1980. Bob Bowman

This species is found only in the North Atlantic Ocean. Within the western North Atlantic, the whiteside's main range is from about Cape Cod (with some stragglers to Chesapeake Bay) to Davis Strait and Greenland. It will be met with throughout the study area from spring through early autumn. The waters surrounding Cape Cod are particularly productive in sightings of this dolphin. Whitesides are also notably abundant in the Gulf of St. Lawrence and along the Gaspé Peninsula.

The white-sided dolphin is quite social, and although it may sometimes be seen singly or in small groups, schools of about fifty animals are average and schools up to five hundred or more are fairly common. This was the dolphin most commonly seen in U.S. waters from Cape Hatteras north during the 1979 CETAP survey. Whitesides are often high-spirited, and one of the most memorable events to be experienced in our waters is being surrounded by hundreds of these animals breaching, lobtailing, and

White-sided dolphin. Mt. Desert Rock, Maine, August 1981. Ann Rivers

White-sided dolphin, close-up of head, showing pointed teeth. Steven Katona

sometimes bowriding. Adding to the excitement is the fact that when whitesides are seen, humpback whales and finback whales will often be found nearby, feeding on the same schools of fish that the dolphins are working. Sometimes several dolphins can be seen swimming in formation directly in front of the head or tail of a whale, perhaps playing in the whale's bow wave.

White-sided dolphins are chiefly fish eaters. It is likely that they take any of the common schooling fish, depending on abundance. The stomachs of specimens inspected during summer and early autumn in the Gulf of Maine have included remains of herring, silver hake, smelt, and short-finned squid.

Individuals or schools of white-sided dolphins become stranded on occasion. Some of the most detailed information available on this species was obtained by the New England Aquarium after an analysis of fifty-seven dolphins from a school of about 150 that stranded in Cobscook Bay, Maine, in September 1974. The largest adult male was 8.75 feet (2.67 m) long, 514 pounds (233 kg), and 22 years old. The largest female was 7.75 feet (2.36 m) long, 400 pounds (181 kg), and about 13 years old. The life cycle inferred from that study includes breeding during July and August by males older than 4 to 6 years and longer than 7.5 feet (2.3 m) with females older than 5 to 8 years; 11 months of gestation; birth of calves (length 3.4–4.25 feet, or 1.0–1.3 m) in June and July; and nursing for up to 18 months. Females probably bear a calf every 2 years.

WHITE-BEAKED DOLPHIN
(*Lagenorhynchus albirostris*)

White-beaked Dolphin
size range: 8–10 feet
John R. Quinn

Whale watchers would do better if this animal were named the white-*backed* dolphin, because the salient field mark is the white patch on the side starting just below and behind the dorsal fin and continuing aft up onto the light saddle that covers the animal's back. At sea the two blend together into one large field of white. Another white patch can be seen on the flank forward of the dorsal fin. Light patches above the flippers and forward of the blowhole may also be visible. The upper portions of the rest of the animal are black, and the belly is white. The white of the belly continues forward onto the short beak. The scientific name (Gr. *lagenos*, bottle, + *rhynchus*, nose; L. *albus*, white, + *rostrum*, snout) translates as "white-snouted bottlenose," which is reasonably close to the common name. The white beak can be seen at sea, although it is much less visible than the white back. Some individuals in the western North Atlantic are said to have dark snouts. This dolphin grows to a maximum length of about 10 feet (3 m).

White-beaked dolphins are somewhat less playful than their relatives, white-sided dolphins, but they can still put on a good show of breaching and lobtailing. A loose group of about twenty whitebeaks seen 3 miles east of Cape Ann on May 16, 1982, showed frequent acrobatics and featured several individuals that continually jumped clear of the water, smacking the surface with their flukes upon reentry while describing a circle. We suspected that fish were being herded to the middle of the circle by the fluke-smacking.

This species is found only in the North Atlantic Ocean, and it may be more common in European than American waters. The western North Atlantic range extends from about Cape Cod to Davis Strait and Greenland. Groups of several to a dozen or two may be encountered throughout our study area, but herds of up to 1,500 occur in the Gulf of St. Lawrence or Newfoundland. Within the Gulf of Maine, waters from Cape Cod to Cape Ann yield sightings from April through November. This species is said to have been

White-beaked dolphin, close-up of head. Newfoundland, 1976.
Judy Perkins

White-beaked dolphins, showing white beaks and white backs. Old Scant-ums Ledge, Maine, May 21, 1977. Steven Katona

White-beaked dolphin breaching. Mingan Islands, Gulf of St. Lawrence, summer 1980. Richard Sears

more common around Cape Cod in the 1950s than at present, and the apparent decline in number of sightings of white-beaks has been accompanied by an increase in sightings of white-sided dolphins. Gulf of Maine records also exist for Mt. Desert Rock (September) and the Bay of Fundy. The Gulf of St. Lawrence, Newfoundland, and Labrador have records of white-beaked dolphins from May to November. The range of this species is somewhat more northerly than that of the whitesides, and its diet may be slightly different. White-beaked dolphins may take more squid (Newfound-landers call them "squidhounds"), but they also take cod, capelin, and other fish or crustaceans. Although the two dolphin species may be found together on occasion, there is some suggestion that their populations are separated seasonally or spatially by water temperatures and ecologically by diet. Information on reproduction and growth rate is not yet available for white-beaked dolphins.

White-beaked dolphin swimming underwater near boat in Newfoundland waters. Gay Alling

COMMON DOLPHIN
(Delphinus delphis)

Common Dolphin
size range: 6–8 feet
John R. Quinn

The scientific name of this species (Gr. *delphis*, dolphin) and its common name both refers to the worldwide abundance of this animal in the warmer waters of all oceans. We can be sure that the sight of thousands of these lovely, slender dolphins leaping and dashing from up to a mile away toward a ship to bowride has gladdened the hearts of sailors for thousands of years, because many of the dolphins figured in Greek and Roman art and writing belonged to this species.

The common dolphin's western North Atlantic range is from Venezuela and the Gulf of Mexico to Newfoundland. The bulk of the population is located in a broad band over the edge of the continental shelf where water temperatures are above 40°F (4.4°C) and where the depth is 100 to 1,000 fathoms. There schools of up to five hundred or one thousand animals (average about fifty) feed on a variety of fishes and squid.

Within our study area, common dolphins should be looked for during offshore passage in the Gulf of Maine seaward of Georges or Browns bank; and at sea off Nova Scotia and Newfoundland, where they occur rather commonly and usually in groups ranging from fifty to more than two hundred. Common dolphins are fast, energetic swimmers that frequently jump clear of the water and also bowride for long periods or play in the wake of a ship. At those times it is easy to see the main field mark of the species, which is a distinct crisscross pattern on the sides. At close range the forward half of the crisscross is seen to be tawny yellow or brown and the posterior half gray. Even if the whole flank cannot be seen, the black "point" below the dorsal fin makes identification easy. In some places this dolphin is called the "saddleback." Bowriding common dolphins sometimes turn on their sides, apparently to look up at the ship, giving one the opportunity to see their striking patterning close-up. The long, pointed snout, black

Common dolphin. The small rectangular blotch midway between the flipper and dorsal fin is a scar. Michael Payne, Manomet Bird Observatory

eye mask, and black stripe from flipper to jaw will be seen clearly.

Although the biology of this species has not been investigated in detail on our side of the Atlantic, information from other locations indicates that females give birth to one calf each year after 11 months of gestation. Calves nurse for 4 months, attain puberty at about 3 years (female) or 4 years (male), and may live for 25 to 30 years. The average adult size is about 7.5 feet (2.3 m), and the maximum size is 8.5 feet (2.6 m). The food ration for an adult common dolphin is about 10 to 20 pounds (4.5–9 kg) per day.

Common dolphin, 1.94 m female. Corolla, North Carolina, March 1, 1975. James G. Mead

STRIPED DOLPHIN
(Stenella coeruleoalba)

*Striped Dolphin
size range: 6–8 feet*
John R. Quinn

Like the common dolphin, the striped dolphin is distributed throughout the warmer waters of all oceans, generally in deep water. It is not common in our study area and normally would be seen only from vessels far offshore or else as stranded specimens. Its western North Atlantic range is from the Gulf of Mexico and the Caribbean to western Greenland. Offshore of the U.S. coast, striped dolphins were found by the 1979 CETAP survey to be most abundant over continental slope waters 100 to 1,000 fathoms deep, especially in the region east of Delaware Bay and Chesapeake Bay. Within the Gulf of Maine, the species is represented mainly by individuals that have stranded along Cape Cod. Striped dolphins are only rarely encountered

97

Striped dolphin stranded on September 18, 1972, at Montauk Point, Montauk, N.Y., showing long snout, pointed teeth, and forward portion of "bilge stripe." American Museum of Natural History Specimen No. 237503. Kevin McCann

in eastern Canadian waters, where records exist for Cape Breton Island, Nova Scotia, and for Sable Island, St. Pierre Bank, and Newfoundland's Placentia Bay.

For identification at sea, the first feature to note is the pale blaze that sweeps from the flank back and up toward the dorsal fin. Next look for the "bilge stripe," a black line running along the light lower flank from the eye to the anus. Although the species takes its common name from that stripe, it is easily visible at sea only when the dolphins jump. Fortunately for observers, striped dolphins often clear the water in fast, low jumps as they speed along in schools of up to a few hundred animals (average size fifty to sixty) and they also are reported to bowride on occasion.

The genus name (Gr. *stenos*, narrow) refers to the long, slender beak, while the species name derives from the Latin for "blue-white," because the first specimen described was supposedly blue above and light below. Such coloring is apparently very unusual, and most live specimens are brown or gray.

The biology of this species in the western North Atlantic is poorly known. In the waters around Japan, where large schools are hunted for food, the life cycle has been detailed as follows. Males and females mature sexually at about 5 to 9 years of age and lengths of 7.2 feet (2.2 m). Females may begin to reproduce shortly thereafter, but males may have to wait for up to 4 or 5 more years for opportunities to mate. Mating males and females can be found together in "mating schools" averaging about 225 animals during the three mating seasons: January–February, May–June, and September–October. The rest of the population remains in larger non-mating schools averaging about 750 dolphins. Fertilized females gestate for 12 months, then bear a single calf slightly over 3 feet (91 cm) long. By 6 months after birth, the calf begins to hunt and eat some prey, but it continues to nurse until weaning at age 1½ years. For up to another 1½ years the calf apparently stays in the mating school with its mother. At about age 2 to 3 juveniles join together into immature schools, where they will remain until about age 5. Individuals then join adult non-mating schools over the next several years. Females are thought to give birth every 3 years. Fish, shrimp, and squid are the main foods of striped dolphins in Japanese waters.

Striped dolphin, 2.16 m female. Fire Island, New York, May 9, 1974. James G. Mead

BOTTLENOSE DOLPHIN
(Tursiops truncatus)

Bottlenose Dolphin
size range: 8–12 feet
John R. Quinn

One of the most familiar and best-loved of all marine mammals is the bottlenose dolphin. As a result of its abundance in temperate to tropical inshore waters throughout the world, its good survival and trainability in captivity, its apparently high intelligence, and its playful, acrobatic nature, this animal has been a favorite display in many oceanaria. Other bottlenose dolphins have appeared in television shows or movies, while some have been trained to assist divers.

Unfortunately, bottlenose dolphins are not common in the cold waters of our study area. They are inhabitants of coastal and inshore waters from Cape Hatteras south along the U.S. coast to Florida and west through the Gulf of Mexico. An offshore population of slightly larger body size is common along the edge of the continental shelf up to New Jersey in winter and Georges Bank in warmer months.

Many people are familiar with the appearance of this animal as a result of aquarium performances or films. Nevertheless, identification at sea is not so easy, because bottlenose dolphins do not routinely do tricks, nor do they often show the short-beaked, "smiling" head. Instead, one must look for the following characteristics. The robust, powerful body may be drab bluish gray or brownish above and slightly lighter below; it lacks a distinct color pattern, but has subtle traces of pigment that can only be seen up close. CETAP aerial survey crews have recently found that offshore bottlenose dolphins have light flank markings similar to those of the *Stenella* species, sweeping up toward the dorsal fin from above the flippers. Such markings could help to reveal whether the few individuals seen north of Cape Cod, most of which are stranded specimens, might have originated from the coastal or the offshore arm of the population. The dorsal fin is similar to that of other dolphins, although a bit thicker and more blunt. Bottlenose dolphins swim in small groups of several to perhaps fifteen animals. At sea they sometimes have been seen schooling with pilot whales.

Bottlenose dolphins hunt bottom fishes, squid, and invertebrates of many different kinds. A list of what they don't eat might be shorter than a list of foods they are known to consume. The daily ration is about 10 percent of the body weight. Depending on the situation, bottlenose dolphins may hunt single prey; team up to herd fish; approach fishing boats to take scraps or discards; steal fish from fishermen's hooks; and even chase fish up salt marsh creeks and onto dry land. As might be guessed from the range of feeding strategies they employ and the variety of tricks they can learn in captivity, bottlenose dolphins have one of the most diverse behavioral repertoires known in the animal kingdom. A large body of information is available on topics including echolocation and acoustic communication, cooperative and help-giving behavior, play, mimicry, courtship and sexual behavior, and learning. Probably more is known about the physiology and anatomy of bottlenose dolphins than about any other cetacean. Suggestions for further reading on these topics are listed in the Bibliography.

Significant events in the life cycle of the bottlenose dolphin include mating during spring and perhaps autumn by sexually mature females about 7.5 feet (2.3 m) long and 5 to 12 years old with males 8 feet (2.4 m) long and 10 to 13 years old; birth of a single calf 3 feet (91 cm) long and weighing about 25 pounds (11.4 kg) every other year after 12 months of gestation; and nursing for 12 to 18 months. A hardy, lucky calf might grow to at least 10 feet (3 m) and 450 pounds (205 kg) and live to 25 to 35 years of age. Lengths to 14 feet (4.3 m) have been recorded. As with many porpoises and other mammals, the teeth get worn down as an animal gets older. The first bottlenose dolphin described scientifically had short, worn-down teeth, so it was given a Latin name derived from *tursio*, porpoise, and *truncatus*, cut off or shortened.

Bottlenose dolphins at Institute for Delphinid Research, Grassy Key, Fla., January 1982. Steven Katona

Bottlenose dolphins jumping during performance at Flipper Sea School, Key West, Fla., January 1982. Steven Katona

GRAY GRAMPUS
(*Grampus griseus*)

Gray Grampus
size range: 9–13 feet
John R. Quinn

The few specimens of this species reported in our study area are strays from warmer waters offshore and south. In such habitats, where water depth is 100 fathoms or more, the gray grampus is common worldwide. The CETAP 1979 survey found this species most common along the continental slope from south of Cape Cod to Cape Hatteras, with some suggestion of northward movement during warmer months. Although few records exist for this species in eastern Canada, one reference notes that large schools have been seen in Newfoundland, where an unsuccessful attempt was made to catch them in the pilot whale fishery. The grampuses could not be herded easily.

The word *grampus* is a corruption of the French words *grand*, big, and *poisson*, fish. In the past, several odontocetes have been called "grampus," but now the term is reserved for

Gray grampus breaching, showing contrast between dark fin and lighter, scratch-marked body. Off Baja California, January 29, 1976. Steven Katona

Gray grampus, showing contrast between dark dorsal fin and lighter body. Off Baja California, January 29, 1976. Steven Katona

Gray grampus, stranded at Monomoy Island, Massachusetts, August 1979. Bob Prescott

Gray grampus, 2.9 m male. Bodie Island, North Carolina, February 11, 1976. James G. Mead

Gray grampus, dark dorsal fin contrasting with lighter scratched body. Richard Rowlett

Grampus griseus. This species is also known as Risso's dolphin because the specimen first described scientifically was collected at Nice, France, in 1811 by an amateur naturalist named Giovanni Risso.

Despite the nondescript common name, these "big gray fish" can usually be distinguished quite easily at sea. They will be encountered in schools of up to thirty animals, although the average size is twenty. They might first be spotted by their acrobatics, for breaching, cartwheeling, lobtailing, and spyhopping are commonly seen. Although they could not be distinguished from other dolphins by length—they average 10 feet (3 m) and 650 pounds (295 kg), with a maximum of 13–14 feet (3.9–4.3 m)—or shape of dorsal fin, their acquired color pattern is usually diagnostic. The gray back and sides nearly always bear numerous white scratches, which may be tooth marks suffered in fights with other gray grampuses or may be inflicted by suckers or beaks of squid. As the scars accumulate, the body and head continue to lighten, emphasizing the contrast with the dark dorsal fin. The bulbous forehead is divided by a shallow vertical furrow that is unique to this species. There is no beak. The sharp demarcation between the black of the lower jaw and the white of the chest can often be seen. Many individuals sport a "necklace" of round light scars or blotches running across the thorax just aft of the flippers.

Relatively little is known about the natural history of the gray grampus. Its main food is thought to be squid. Like a number of other squid eaters (including the sperm whale, the pygmy sperm whale, and the various beaked whales), the grampus normally has teeth only in the lower jaw. Individuals may have from two to seven pairs of teeth, the average being three or four pairs located at the front of the lower jaw.

KILLER WHALE
(Orcinus orca)

Killer Whale
size range: male, up to 30 feet;
female, up to 22 feet
John R. Quinn

This striking and beautiful medium-sized whale is well known to the North American public as a result of media attention during the past decade. The bold, crisp black-and-white pattern that is so attractive to designers also makes a killer whale very easy to spot and identify at sea. The most visible feature at a distance is the extraordinarily tall swordlike dorsal fin of adult males, which may reach 6 feet (1.8 m) or more in height. The dorsal fins of females and juveniles are smaller and curved and more closely resemble the fins of other dolphins. The distinctive field mark to look for is the oval white patch above and behind each eye. At close range the white of the abdomen can be seen to extend partway up the rear flank, and a gray "saddle" is visible right behind the dorsal fin.

Killer whales are found in all oceans of the world, but

they are most common in cooler waters and in productive coastal areas. The normal social unit is a group (called a "pod") of up to twenty whales of both sexes and all ages, made up largely of relatives. Individual whales can be distinguished by differences in fin shape, including nicks and scars caused by various injuries, and by differences in the shape of the gray saddle. Using such distinguishing features, group composition and home range have been studied in detail over a period of years in the Pacific Northwest. Pods are enduring social units that maintain their cohesiveness and inhabit the same home range for many years, much as do the matriarchal social groups of African elephants.

Much less is known about killer whales in the western North Atlantic. They are clearly a regular component of our cetacean fauna, as some dozens of sightings or strandings have been recorded, mainly from about New Jersey to Labrador. Yet reports of sightings are not as common as one

Killer whale, half breach. Mt. Desert Island, Maine, June 1982. Scott Marion

Killer whale, blowhole open, showing diagnostic white patch above and behind eye. Mt. Desert Island, Maine, June 1982. Scott Marion

might expect, considering the frequency with which killer whale tooth marks occur on humpback whale flukes. Furthermore, understanding of any migration paths in our region is poor. Within the Gulf of Maine, killer whale sightings are most common from about mid-July to September on Jeffreys Ledge and between the Isles of Shoals and Provincetown. Fishermen in those waters have observed killer whale attacks on bluefin tuna, and it may be that the whales regularly follow parts of the tuna's migrations. Several possible attacks on large whales at Jeffreys Ledge have also been reported to us. However, killer whales also occur in the Gulf of Maine during winter, when tuna and baleen whales are scarce. Two large males shot in the winter of 1902 near Eastport, Maine, were said to be eating herring. A winter stranding also occurred in Minas Basin, Bay of Fundy, in 1950. In eastern Canadian waters, the movements of killer whales may be more closely linked with the distribution of other whales on which they prey. Scientists summarizing Maritimes sightings as of 1957 suggested that killer whales followed the movements of rorqual whales through the area in spring and early summer, passing the east coast of Newfoundland in June and the Strait of Belle Isle in June and July, with some continuing along Labrador and into the Arctic. Scientists from Memorial University of Newfoundland observed killer whales attacking humpback whales on the Grand Bank in July 1982. Killer whales are also said to have preyed on beluga whales in the St. Lawrence River estuary during spring and autumn. It seems a little unlikely that all of these records (and others) can be fitted into one migration path, and it would not be surprising if several different groups of killer whales inhabited our study area.

Although no data on reproduction are available for our study area, information from a variety of locations has been used to form a preliminary model of the cycle. Males mature sexually at about 19–22 feet (5.8–6.7 m), compared with about 16 feet (4.9 m) for females. Age at sexual maturity is poorly known. Males can grow to about 30 feet (9.1 m) and at least 8 tons (7.2 metric tons) and females to perhaps 26 feet (7.9 m) and 4 or 5 tons (3.6–4.5 metric tons), although both may be somewhat smaller in our study area.

Males in pods may fertilize more than one female during the late autumn to midwinter mating season. Single calves about 8 feet (2.4 m) long weighing 375 pounds (170 kg) are born after a long pregnancy, estimated at 12 to 16 months. Nursing lasts for at least 2 years, and the length at weaning may be about 13 feet (4 m). The interval between calves appears to be very long, up to 7 years or more. The overall birth rate for the Pacific Northwest population may be about 4–5 percent per year, with natural mortality about the same. Maximum longevity may be as high as 35 or 40 years.

These whales are opportunistic feeders on a diverse range of food items, including fish, squid, birds, seals, and baleen whales at various times and places. Tuna and herring are thought to be important foods in the Gulf of Maine, and herring has also been named as a principal food for killer whales in Icelandic waters. Baleen whales, including minkes and perhaps young finbacks or humpbacks, are

Killer whale, one of a pair of 25-foot males shot in Eastport, Maine, March 1902. F. W. True

thought to be important foods in eastern Canada and on occasion in the Gulf of Maine. A killer whale's daily food intake is about 4 percent of its body weight. It seems likely that the social structure of killer whales is mainly an adaptation to hunting large whales. Observations of their attacks on rorqual whales have emphasized the use of strategy, group coordination, and cooperation in herding and subduing animals many times their size. Although small groups of killer whales have also demonstrated those traits while herding fish or ambushing seals, it would seem that small prey could routinely be obtained by individuals, as is the case with other odontocetes. The evolution of stable, long-lived pods; the long period of calf dependency on the mother (presumably accompanied by learning); large size; long lifetime; and relatively high intelligence would all be useful adaptations for producing experienced, integrated teams of animals able to tackle the largest, most powerful prey on earth. Several phonograph recordings that include echolocation and communication sounds of killer whales are listed in the Bibliography.

Some of the behavior traits mentioned above have been responsible for the success of captive killer whales as popular exhibits in many seaquaria. They are easily trained, cooperative, and even gentle and affectionate to their trainers. Although it is sad to see individuals denied the opportunity to range freely through the ocean, their performances undoubtedly have contributed to the strength of the whale protection movement, and the knowledge gained from observing them closely has contributed to a better understanding of their species. These whales are no longer perceived as fierce killers of the sea, keen to devour man or beast, and thus many people prefer to call them "orcas" rather than killer whales. Ironically, that might translate loosely as "devil whale," since Orcus was the Roman god of the underworld. Although there is no indication that killer whales bear any malice toward people or have ever intentionally harmed a human swimmer, there are several unexplained accounts of boats being rammed and sunk by

Killer whale, full breach. Stellwagen Bank, May 15, 1982. Lyda Phillips

them. Perhaps it would be useful to compare these animals to wolves or lions, which have evolved similar social structures and behavioral traits for the same reason—to be able to take large prey. These species deserve our respect as animals exquisitely adapted to be efficient social hunters, and we need not invest them with more gentleness than they have, or than we had during that stage in our own evolutionary history.

Killer whale flukes. Mt. Desert Island, June 1982.
Bob Bowman

Jaws of killer whale, National Museum of Natural History, Smithsonian Institution, Specimen 11980. Carey Bell

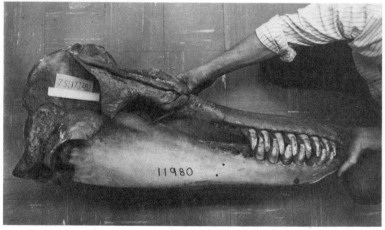

Male killer whale. Newfoundland coast, summer 1977. Peter Cohen (ORES)

BELUGA
(Delphinapterus leucas)

Beluga Whale
size range: 10–15 feet
John R. Quinn

Whale watchers in our study area are uniquely fortunate to be able to view a small population of these "white whales" in the St. Lawrence River estuary, rather than having to travel to the remote shores of their primary habitat in Hudson Bay, Greenland, and the arctic coasts of Canada, Alaska, and the Soviet Union. The St. Lawrence population, estimated variably at 325 animals or 500 to 1,000 animals, is almost certainly a separate stock from the several thousand belugas that inhabit inshore waters of the subarctic and arctic coast of eastern Canada and the 5,000 to 10,000 whales that inhabit Hudson Bay. The St. Lawrence River population may be declining, since up to 5,000 belugas are said to have been present during the early part of the century. Throughout their arctic range, belugas have been and still are important sources of meat, fat, and oil for Eskimos.

Even whale watchers who don't go to the St. Lawrence River may someday see a free-living beluga, because a few make their way south following cold currents around Nova

Scotia and into the Bay of Fundy, or down the U.S. coast as far as Long Island. One or two belugas entering U.S. coastal waters every few years would hardly be noticeable if the animals were not pure white and inclined to come close to shore, swim into weirs, or feed near fishing boats. Although these animals are adapted to life in cold seas, strays can apparently survive and feed in those warmer waters, perhaps for several years. Belugas have been kept successfully for years at several aquariums.

Adult belugas range from about 11 feet (3.4 m) for females to 13 feet (4 m) for males. The pure white adult color may allow the whale to hide from predators among ice floes and may also reduce the rate of heat loss from the body. If the white color of adult belugas is adaptive, it is hard to understand why beluga calves are born dark gray or brown, lightening only slowly to become white in about the tenth year of life. Other adaptations for life in freezing seas can also be seen. Absence of a dorsal fin (the scientific name means "white finless dolphin") would reduce heat loss and avoid abrasion by ice. On top of a beluga's head the skin is very thick and its blubber is thin, probably so that the whale can ram through several inches of ice, when necessary, to make a breathing hole. Navigation under ice fields or through floating ice packs probably demands frequent use of sonar to detect obstacles or scattered breathing holes. A beluga's neck vertebrae are not fused together, and the relatively free movement of its short-beaked, round-meloned head may be useful for navigating in the presence of ice. Communication between animals for navigation, hunting, or other purposes involves high-pitched trills, squeals, and whistles. Those sounds can be heard through the hull of a boat and have led to the beluga's local name, "sea canary."

The beluga's reproductive cycle is particularly interesting. Females mature sexually at age 4 to 7 years and males at age 8 to 9. Mating takes place in spring or early summer. The following summer, after about 14 months of pregnancy, the female will join large numbers of other pregnant females, plus males, in shallow water at the mouths of

Beluga in Cape Cod Canal, 1971. Barry T. O'Neil

arctic creeks and rivers. There, in relatively warm water
(50°–60°F, or 10°–15°C), females give birth to single calves,
each 4 to 5 feet (1.2–1.5 m) long and about 75 to 100
pounds (34–45 kg). The temperature advantage gained in
these sheltered estuaries benefits the small calves until they
put on additional blubber from nursing. Calves are completely dependent on nursing for a year, supplement
mother's milk during the second year with food caught by
hunting, and are weaned at age 2. Maximum longevity may
be more than 25 years. A female will bear one calf every
2 or 3 years.

Within the St. Lawrence region, belugas calve and mate
during spring in small bays and estuaries around the
Saguenay River and around some islands. Their main

summer distribution includes the St. Lawrence estuary and the northern (Iles aux Coudres to Pointe des Monts) and southern (Rivière Ouelle to Rimouski) coasts of the Gulf of St. Lawrence. During warm months the whales approach the coast at high tide. In September and October, numbers of belugas can be seen near Les Escoumins, among other places. In winter they are restricted by ice to open water at the mouth of the Saguenay River and eastward to Les Escoumins. The usual size of beluga pods is two to twenty-five animals, but groups of up to two hundred have been seen.

Belugas migrating north along Arctic coast of Alaska, showing finless back and white body. The immature animal in the middle is slightly darker. April 1973. Chester Beachell, courtesy National Film Board of Canada

Belugas have a diverse, opportunistic diet that includes many species of fish, squid, crabs, shrimp, clams, and worms, all taken near the bottom in relatively shallow water during dives of up to about 21 fathoms.

The beluga presents zoologists with an interesting puzzle. Its body features clearly demonstrate adaptation to arctic conditions, yet individuals seem able to survive and to feed in warmer waters. Why then are belugas limited mainly to arctic waters? Although we may never know with certainty, it seems likely that competition for food in more southerly areas from well-established populations of harbor porpoises, harbor seals, and gray seals in coastal waters and white-sided dolphins, white-beaked dolphins, and pilot whales (among others) in offshore waters might be an important factor. Predation by sharks, which are more numerous in warm waters, might also help to limit the beluga's range.

SPERM WHALE
(Physeter catodon)

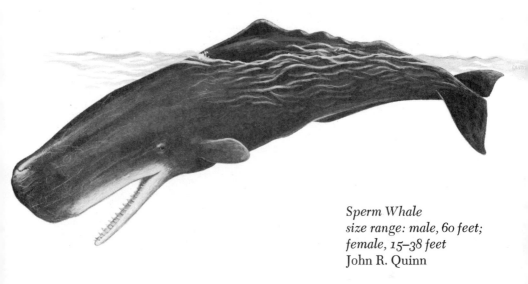

Sperm Whale
size range: male, 60 feet;
female, 15–38 feet
John R. Quinn

Sperm whales, immortalized in *Moby Dick*, and the mainstay of the great American whaling fleet during the eighteenth and nineteenth centuries, are the largest of the toothed whales. Males may reach a length of 60 feet (18 m), although a size of 50 feet (15 m) and 48 tons (43 metric tons) is more common. Females are a good deal smaller, reaching only 38 feet (11.6 m) and 15 tons (13.5 metric tons).

Few people would have any difficulty identifying this species, given a good look, as it is one of the most distinctive and bizarre animals on earth. Unfortunately, the massive, blunt head, which is fully one-third the length of a large male, and the long, narrow, underslung lower jaw are usually not fully visible at sea. Identification must then be made on the following characteristics. The single nostril is located on the left side of the front of the head, and the 15-foot-tall (4.5-m) spout is therefore tipped forward and

123

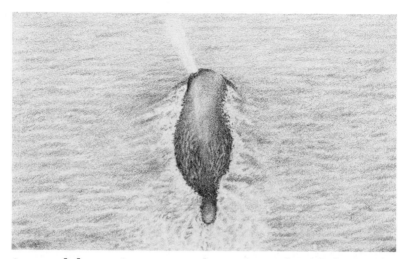

Sperm whale seen from rear, single spout tipped forward and left.
D. D. Tyler

to the left at an angle of about 45°. The dorsal fin is usually only a low hump, which is followed by a series of bumps along the ridge of the back and tail. Sperm whales are usually slate gray or brownish, and the skin on the flanks is usually noticeably wrinkled or corrugated. The flukes, usually shown as the whale dives, are large and triangular, with smooth edges, rounded tips, and a deep central notch. The scientific name (Gr. *physa*, bellows, and G. *kata*, inferior, + *odontos*, tooth) translates roughly as "spouter with teeth on the bottom," emphasizing that functional teeth are present only in the sperm whale's lower jaw.

One might wish for more opportunities to identify sperm whales than would be encountered in most parts of our study area. Sperm whales prefer deep water and generally stay along the edge of the continental shelf in water 500 or 1,000 fathoms deep or farther out to sea. In such habitats the species ranges throughout the world's oceans and from the Equator to high latitudes, pursuing the squid that form its chief food.

Each day a large male sperm whale will eat about 3.5 percent of its body weight in squid. Although fish and other items are occasionally taken, it is the search for squid that accounts for much of the behavior and biology of sperm whales. Many other cetaceans hunt squid, often in the same locations as do sperm whales, but the evolution of extraordinary adaptations has allowed this species to escape competition by feeding at depths far beyond those attainable by any other mammal. We may never know all the factors that allow sperm whales to hunt routinely at depths of up to 250 fathoms and on occasion at depths of nearly a mile (1.6 km) or more, but the following scenario blends old whaling lore and current findings.

Old whalermen observed that sperm whales come up about where they dive, which suggests that they do not swim around much while feeding. They also knew that a sperm whale would, on average, take one breath for each foot (30 cm) of its body length and would then dive one minute for each foot of length. Thus a 45-foot (13.7-m) whale would dive for 45 minutes, come up in the same place, and breathe about forty-five times before its next dive. Recent research suggests that sperm whales initially

Removal of stranded sperm whale from freezing waters at Rockport, Maine, March 1976, for transport to New England Aquarium. Note wrinkled skin. Steven Katona

Sperm whale stranded at Cape Cod. Nedra Foster Hecker

locate squid using powerful sonar pulses that sound like the banging of a carpenter's hammer. Each whale's sonar pulse rhythm is individually distinctive, and school members maintain acoustic contact while diving. After reaching a depth where squid are abundant, the whales may remain motionless and lure the squid to them. The huge reservoir of waxy liquid in the whale's head may be used as a buoyancy regulator. To decrease buoyancy, the whale reduces blood circulation to the spermaceti organ, then pumps cold sea water in through the blowhole, cooling and congealing some of the wax. To increase buoyancy, the whale reliquefies the wax by allowing blood from the body core to reenter the spermaceti organ. Old whalers thought that the wax was a whale's sperm, so they called it "spermaceti" and the whale "sperm whale." Luring the squid to the motionless whale might be done as follows. No sunlight penetrates to the depth where a sperm whale feeds, but many squid, fishes, and crustaceans at those depths are luminescent. If a sperm whale caught and ate a luminescent squid, its white lips and teeth might glow from some of the luminescent secretions adhering to them. If the whale hung weightlessly and silently in the water with its glowing mouth open, other squid might come close enough to be engulfed. Most of the

Sockets in upper jaw of female sperm whale stranded at Seawall, Mt. Desert Island, Maine, October 21, 1966. Paul Favour

Lower jaw and teeth of whale in the above photo. Paul Favour

en are only several feet long, but giant squid up to
(9 m) long have been found in sperm whales'
s, and sucker-inflicted scars found on some whales
ness to battles with truly enormous squid, perhaps
100 feet (30 m) long.

The social structure of sperm whale populations is complex. Females, including those which are pregnant or nursing, calves, and some juveniles swim in groups called "mixed schools" or "nursery schools," averaging about twenty-five animals in size. After weaning, young males may form "juvenile schools." When males reach puberty at about age 9, they may join "bachelor schools" of up to ten whales. During the breeding season in spring and early summer, large males compete for control of sexually mature females, which are normally over 28 feet (8.5 m), 7 tons (6.3 metric tons), and 8 years old. Successful males obtain exclusive breeding rights to "harems" averaging ten females. Battles over females probably occur, judging from the sperm whale tooth marks that scar the skin of most males. Even though males achieve sexual maturity at 39 feet long (11.9 m), 20 tons (18 metric tons), and 19 years of age, a male probably has no opportunity to breed until he achieves "social maturity" by deposing a reigning harem-master bull in battle. Harem masters are usually over 45 feet long (13.7 m), 30 tons (27 metric tons), and 25 years of age. Large old bulls without harems swim singly or in small groups throughout the year, venturing during summer into the cold water of high latitudes, while females and young sperm whales generally stay within the area from 45° south to 45° north latitude.

The reproductive rate of this species is one of the slowest for all whales. Gestation lasts about 15 months and the 13-foot (4-m), 2,200-pound (998-kg) calf nurses for 2 years, during which time it will grow to 22 feet (6.7 m) and about 3 tons (2.7 metric tons). A female probably does not become pregnant for at least another 9 months after weaning ends; thus the rate of calving is about once every 4 years. Awareness of the slow reproductive rate and un-certainty about the effects on reproduction of changes in sex ratios and population structure caused by hunting led the International Whaling Commission to pass a zero quota resolution, under which no sperm whales will be caught anywhere for three years starting in 1981.

Most readers of this guide will not be able to get out to the continental slope and beyond to see some of the tens of thousands of sperm whales that remain in the North Atlantic despite periods of Yankee whaling during the 1800s and modern whaling by Canada, Iceland, and other nations. The 1979 CETAP census estimate for the sperm whale population in U.S. coastal waters north of Cape Hatteras and out to 500 fathoms depth was a minimum of three hundred animals. Only on rare occasions will one or a few sperm whales swim into shallower waters over the continental shelf, perhaps following squid schools during their onshore-offshore migrations. The few records for the Gulf of Maine include a 31-foot (9.4-m) female that stranded alive on Mt. Desert Island, October 20, 1966; an orphaned 15-foot (4.5-m), 3,000-pound (1,360-kg) un-weaned male found alive at Rockport, Maine, on March 22, 1976, which was trucked to the New England Aquarium and provided with intensive care, but which died there of pneumonia on March 26; and a single sperm whale observed halfway between Grand Manan Island, New Brunswick, and Nova Scotia by New England Aquarium scientists in October 1981. Sperm whales are also rare in the Gulf of St. Lawrence, although several single sightings or strandings have occurred there. They are more commonly seen offshore from Nova Scotia and Newfoundland, where large males used to be taken by the fishery.

PYGMY SPERM WHALE
(Kogia breviceps)

*Pygmy Sperm Whale
size range: 9–13 feet*
John R. Quinn

This small whale, which occurs in warm waters of the Atlantic, Pacific, and Indian oceans, is very rare in our study area. Two live pygmy sperm whales stranded just south of our area at West Yarmouth, Mass., on Nantucket Sound on December 26, 1982. The sole record for the Gulf of Maine is of a dead individual at Nahant, Mass., in 1910. Two dead specimens have been found in eastern Canada, one at Sable Island in 1969 and the other under ice in Halifax harbor, Nova Scotia, during the winter of 1970. It is not known whether any of those animals came ashore alive. The Nova Scotian strandings are the northernmost records published for the species. Very few reports of live sightings of pygmy sperm whales at sea exist anywhere. CETAP aerial surveys did observe one beyond the continental shelf edge off the coast of New Jersey in 1981. In view of the paucity of live sightings, it is surprising to find that strandings of pygmy sperm whales are very common along tropical and subtropical shores. Records of the Scientific Event Alert Network show that pygmy sperm whales are one of the most frequently stranded cetacean species along the southeast U.S. coastline. Most of the data available on these animals thus comes from dead specimens outside our study area, and the following information is

Pygmy sperm whale, 2.6 m female, showing tiny underslung lower jaw and false gill mark. Virginia Beach, Virginia, December 12, 1975. James G. Mead

provided more in the hope of whetting zoological curiosity than with the expectation that many readers will see this species.

The average adult size of a pygmy sperm whale is about 10 feet (3 m) and 800 pounds (362 kg). The color is gray above, light below, supposedly with a pinkish tinge when the animal is alive. A small dorsal fin is set toward the rear of the back. The head, which is only about one-seventh the body length, and its underslung lower jaw put one in mind of a shark just as much as of a sperm whale. The species name, from the Greek *brevis*, short, and *cepitis*, head, is descriptive. Some drawings and photographs of the animal show a light crescent exactly in the place where a large fish would have a gill slit. If such a mark is common, one might consider the possibility that pygmy sperm whales capitalize on their sharklike appearance for some degree of protection from real sharks. Similarities to the sperm whale's appearance include having teeth only in the lower jaw and displacement of the blowhole slightly forward and to the left of the normal odontocete position. Furthermore, the head contains a small spermaceti organ.

The few observations that have been made on pygmy sperm whales at sea are of exceptional interest. These whales apparently occur individually or in small schools of up to perhaps six animals. They are said to be very easy to approach, lying quietly at the surface practically until touched, then diving suddenly while defecating a reddish-brown cloud into the water. If such behavior is normal, one must wonder whether the defecated cloud functions as a visual or olfactory decoy during escape behavior. One scientist speculated that the "approachability" of pygmy sperm whales might be one factor in their apparent rarity, since whaling captains might have used them as practice targets for training inexperienced crewmen on the way to the whaling grounds.

Although stranded specimens have yielded up some secrets about pygmy sperm whales—such as the fact that they eat squid, fish, crabs, and shrimps—the speculations above demonstrate how little we know about this pint-sized

Pygmy sperm whale at New England Aquarium, 1980. Specimen MH-80-Kb. Note sharklike head with teeth in lower jaw. Scott Kraus

mystery of the cetacean world. Even the derivation of its genus name is a puzzle, since nobody knows what *Kogia* means. Perhaps it is derived from the Middle English *cog*, a tooth, and refers to the twelve to sixteen pairs of sharp, curved teeth in the lower jaw. However, an obscure meaning of *cog* is a deception or trick, which could refer to the animal's resemblance to a shark.

NORTHERN BOTTLENOSE WHALE
(*Hyperoodon ampullatus*)

Bottlenose Whale
size range: male, up to 29 feet;
female, up to 26 feet
John R. Quinn

The family of toothed whales to which this species belongs is known as the Ziphiidae, or "beaked whales." Probably less is known about this group than about any of the families of cetaceans, and perhaps less than about any other family of mammals. The group includes eighteen named species, but it is likely that some species have not yet been described. Some of the named species are known only from one or a few remains of stranded specimens. All of the species share the following characteristics: (1) two distinct grooves on the ventral side of the jaw joining to form a forward-pointing V, (2) a small dorsal fin set toward the rear of the back, and (3) flukes lacking a central notch except in one species. Furthermore, in all species save one there has been an extraordinary reduction of the number of teeth, such that usually only one or two pairs of teeth are located in the lower jaw and no functional teeth are found in the upper jaw. All of the beaked whales appear to feed mainly on squid, and it may be that the major evolutionary theme within this group has been adaptive radiation to feed on different squid at different places in the world ocean.

More information is available about the northern bottlenose whale than about any other beaked whale, largely because it has been commercially hunted for its oil and meat by Scotland, Norway, Iceland, and Canada at various times in the past century. This species is found only in deep arctic and temperate waters of the North Atlantic Ocean. Historical catches provide a measure of its recent abundance. Over 14,000 were taken east of Greenland between 1890 and 1896 and nearly 26,000 between 1890 and 1900. More than 3,000 animals were taken annually in several of those years. Over time the fishery was extended westward into Newfoundland waters. From 1938 to 1973 Norway took 4,870 bottlenose whales outside of Norwegian waters. Hunting of this species stopped after 1972, probably because of population decline, but also because Canada closed its whaling stations, England forbade the use of whale meat in pet food, and Norwegian fur farms switched to other foods. The legacy of this hunting appears to be a greatly reduced population of northern bottlenose whales. Although no recent population census is available, the stock is considered to be critically depleted, and a zero quota is in effect. An estimate of at least 28,000 bottlenose whales for the North Atlantic as of 1965 was calculated from the cumulative catches made between 1965 and 1971. An interesting zoological question is why this species has been numerous enough to support a whaling industry when so many of the other beaked whales are apparently very rare.

Although bottlenose whales are usually found in cold, deep water, whale watchers in our study area are fortunate to have a place where this medium-sized whale can be seen with some regularity. Even though that location is far offshore, some of the cruises run by Ocean Research Education Society and Sea Education Association (see Appendix II for addresses) do visit the site, known as the Gully, off Sable Island, and do sometimes encounter these whales. Canadian whalers took eighty-seven bottlenose whales from the Gully and the edge of the Grand Bank between 1962 and 1967.

The species is also well known along the edge of the continental shelf off Newfoundland and Labrador. A live individual was seen at Cape Martin, Gulf of St. Lawrence, in 1940, and two live whales came into Trinity Bay, Newfoundland, in July 1953. No live bottlenose whales have ever been reported at sea in the Gulf of Maine, but a male found on the beach at North Dennis, Mass., in January 1869 may have been alive at or shortly before stranding, and a young male and female were alive when they stranded at Beverly Farms, Mass., in October 1923. The Beverly Farms whales made deep groaning and sobbing sounds that could be heard for a distance of half a mile. A 20-foot (6-m) male was found dead at Cobequid Bay, Bay of Fundy, in October 1969 and described in great detail. The southernmost record for the species on this side of the Atlantic is for a live 27-foot (8.2-m) female at Newport, R.I., in February 1867. The preponderance of autumn and winter dates for these southern strandings and sightings has led Canadian scientists to suspect that bottlenose whales may winter far offshore from the Grand Bank south to about Cape Cod.

While it should be clear that most whale watchers need not worry too much about remembering the field marks for this species, we include the following information for completeness. If these descriptions should stimulate someone to make the necessary arrangements to go see bottlenose whales, or if they lead to a report of a stranding that would otherwise have gone unnoticed, our efforts will be amply repaid.

Male bottlenose whales grow to about 29 feet (8.8 m) and 4 tons (3.6 metric tons); females reach about 26 feet (7.9 m) and 3.5 tons (3.2 metric tons). Observers who have been fortunate enough to encounter them at sea usually describe the color as brown. Smaller animals appear to be a uniform chocolate brown, while larger ones develop varying amounts of light or yellow color. Males, especially, frequently bear scratches and scars over large portions of their bodies, perhaps resulting from combat with other males. In the bottlenose whale, as in many of the other beaked whales, the two teeth are located at the tip of the lower jaw and if used in fighting would probably produce such scarring. The genus name derives from the Greek *hyperoon,* palate, + *odous,* tooth. The first specimen described supposedly had tiny teeth in the palate. Squid-eating odontocetes tend to have roughened palates for holding the slippery prey.

A large, old specimen, especially a male, may develop a cream-colored head and a high, bulging melon. When seen at sea, these whales appear to have a slight, faintly gray depression or "neck" behind the melon. As in all ziphiid whales, the elongation of the jaws is visible externally as a short beak, and this species frequently shows its head and beak when breathing. The species name (L. *ampulla,* a round bottle) refers to the head shape, as does the common name, "bottlenose." The breath is visible as a spout, perhaps 5 feet (1.5 m) tall. Bottlenose whales are most frequently

Bottlenose whale, showing light head and beak, at the Gully, Nova Scotia. Howard E. Winn

seen in small schools of five to fifteen animals, and evidence suggests that there may be a complex social structure. Catching them was made easier by two behavior traits, "curiosity" and "helpfulness." Bottlenose whales commonly approach stationary vessels, especially those with a generator running or some other source of noise. They have also frequently been observed to stay with wounded school members, supporting them at the surface to aid breathing. Both traits contributed to the decline of the species from overhunting. Individuals have also been seen to breach and lobtail. Bottlenose whales feed mainly on squid (especially the deep-sea species *Gonatus fabricii*) but also take herring and bottom invertebrates such as sea stars. Dive times of an hour or more are apparently common, suggesting that the whales feed at great depths. As in the sperm whale, the large, oil-rich melon may be involved in deep diving capability. The strong sexual dimorphism in body size and melon development indicates that males and females may behave somewhat differently. The sexes may segregate seasonally during migrations, and large males may swim to higher latitudes. There is some evidence that large males dominate harems of females during the breeding season in spring and summer.

DENSE-BEAKED WHALE
(*Mesoplodon densirostris*)

Dense-beaked Whale
size range: up to 14 or 16 feet
John R. Quinn

Twelve species of the family Ziphiidae are assigned to the genus *Mesoplodon*. The biology of the group is poorly understood, and some of the species are known only from several stranded specimens. Even experts have great difficulty in identifying these animals precisely on the few occasions when they are seen at sea. We are aware of only one live sighting of a *Mesoplodon* species within our study area; however, three species have been recovered from strandings. For the purposes of this guide it is sufficient to note that most *Mesoplodon* species are oceanic in warm or temperate waters. Squid of various types appear to be the main food. These whales have been observed swimming in small groups of up to six animals. They all appear to be more or less similar in general appearance and size, with average lengths of perhaps 15 feet (4.5 m). All are dark above and lighter beneath, with some body scarring, a small dorsal fin set far back, and no central notch to the flukes. However, the species differ strikingly (and inexplicably) in the size and position of the one or two pairs of teeth in the lower jaw. The

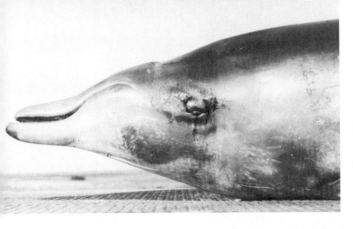

*Dense-beaked whale,
left view of head, 3.97 m
female stranded at
Buxton, North Carolina,
March 4, 1975.* James
G. Mead

genus name (Gr. *mesos*, close to, + *diploos*, double, + *odous*, tooth) means "related to two-toothed whales."

The dense-beaked whale (L. *densus*, dense, + *rostrum*, beak), which has a worldwide distribution in deep tropical and subtropical waters, has been found stranded in our study area at Annisquam, Mass., in 1898; Peggy's Cove, Nova Scotia, in 1940; and most recently at Cape Breton Island, Nova Scotia, in December 1968. This is one of the easier *Mesoplodon* species to identify, because its lower jaw swells to an enormous prominence midway along its length. Each mandibular prominence contains one spectacular tooth 6 to 8 inches (15–20 cm) high, nearly 3 inches (7.5 cm) wide, and nearly 2 inches (5 cm) thick. Only the tip of each tooth protrudes from its socket, and then only in males, whereas in females the entire tooth remains covered by gum tissue. Scientists were able to record chirps and whistles from one dense-beaked whale that came ashore alive in Florida.

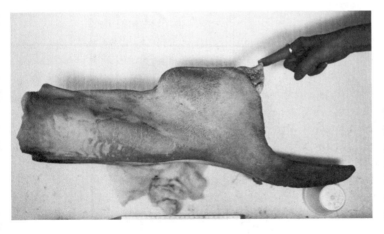

*Right lower jaw of
dense-beaked whale,
showing single tooth in
huge socket. National
Museum of Natural
History Specimen
5SI6JA82.* Carey Bell

TRUE'S BEAKED WHALE
(Mesoplodon mirus)

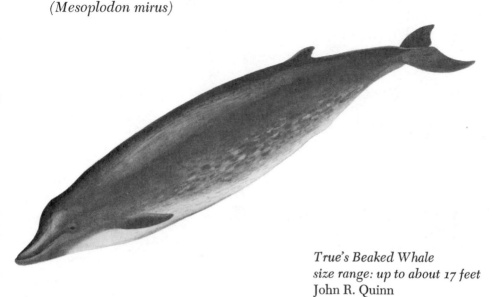

True's Beaked Whale
size range: up to about 17 feet
John R. Quinn

This species is known primarily from temperate waters of both sides of the North Atlantic, although there appears to be another population along the South African coast. The two strandings from our study area occurred at Wells Beach, Maine, in March 1906 and at Ste. Anne's Bay, Cape Breton Island, Nova Scotia, on August 5, 1938. The mandible contains two small, triangular, flattened teeth, located at the very tip of the lower jaw, which only erupt in males. The species name is from the Latin *mirari*, to wonder at, but it is not clear why this beaked whale is more wonderful than the others. It was first described in 1913 by Frederick True, and relatively little has been learned about it since.

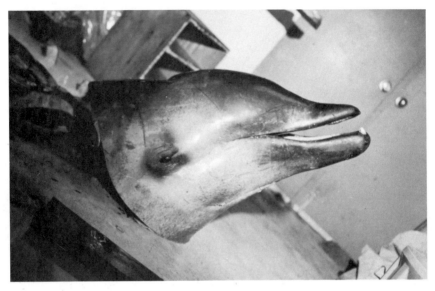

True's beaked whale, right view of head showing teeth at tip of mandible of 4.57 m male stranded at Assateague Island, Maryland, November 3, 1977. James G. Mead

NORTH SEA BEAKED WHALE
(*Mesoplodon bidens*)

North Sea Beaked Whale
size range: up to 16 feet
Sarah Landry

The distribution of this species appears to be centered in the eastern North Atlantic, judging from the thirty or so strandings on European coasts. It ranges further north than other *Mesoplodon* species and seems to inhabit cooler waters and perhaps to enter coastal waters more readily at some seasons for feeding. It is also known as Sowerby's beaked whale, after the man who in 1804 described the first specimen, found in Scotland in 1800. The species name means "two-toothed."

Only four records are known from North America, all from in or near our study area, including one live sighting. The living animal, 14 feet (4.3 m) long and probably a female, was harpooned in Notre Dame Bay, Newfoundland, on September 23, 1953. A dead male, 15.5 feet (4.7 m) long, was found in Trinity Bay, Newfoundland, on August 26, 1952. The other two specimens both came ashore on Nantucket Island, Mass., one in 1867 and the latest on September 16, 1982.

Each side of the lower jaw has one flattened tooth lo-

North Sea beaked whale, 3.96 m female stranded at Colleville, France, September 1975. D. Robineau, courtesy James G. Mead

North Sea beaked whale, close-up of head. Colleville, France, September 1975. D. Robineau, courtesy James G. Mead

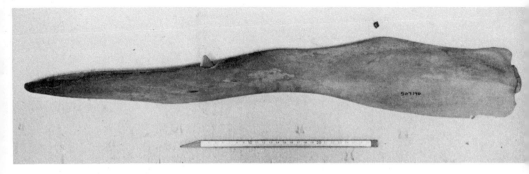

Lower left jaw of North Sea beaked whale, showing single tooth midway along length. Carey Bell

cated midway along the mandible, with its pointed crown directed slightly toward the rear. Enough stranded specimens have been recovered in Europe to show that mating takes place in late winter or spring; gestation lasts about one year; and the 7-foot (2.1-m) calf nurses for about a year until weaning at 10 feet (3 m) long.

Key to Identifying Stranded Whales and Porpoises Found between Cape Cod and Newfoundland

I. Baleen in upper jaw (may be rotted out in dead specimens). No teeth. Double blowhole. Usually over 30 feet long (except minke whales and juveniles). Continue to A. BALEEN WHALES.

II. Baleen absent, teeth present (sometimes under gums). Single blowhole. Much shorter than 30 feet (except sperm and largest killer and bottlenose whales). Continue to B. TOOTHED WHALES.

A. Baleen Whales (Mysticetes)

1. a. Dorsal fin and throat grooves present. Go to 2.
   b. Dorsal fin and throat grooves absent. Length up to 55 feet; arched jaw 25 percent of body length; rough callosities on head; baleen dark, up to 390 plates per side, each up to 7 feet long with up to 175 bristles per inch. RIGHT WHALE.

c. Dorsal fin and throat grooves absent. Length up to 65 feet; huge arched jaw up to 40 percent of body length; no callosities on head; baleen dark, up to 360 plates per side, each up to 15 feet long with up to about 212 bristles per inch; arctic, very rare. BOWHEAD WHALE.

2. a. Over 30 feet long. Go to 3.

   b. Under 30 feet long; 50–70 ventral grooves; up to 325 plates per side of short (8 inches), yellowish or cream-colored baleen with up to 63 bristles per inch; white patch on flipper, pointed snout. MINKE WHALE.

   c. Under 30 feet, but not as in 2b. Juvenile baleen whale. Go to 3.

3. a. Length to 55 feet; up to 25 wide throat grooves reaching to umbilicus; knobby head and jaws; white flipper up to 33 percent of body length; sawtoothed hind edges on flukes; black baleen, up to 400 plates per side, each up to 2.5 feet long, with up to 88 bristles per inch. HUMPBACK WHALE.

   b. Shorter flippers, smooth edges on flukes, over 25 throat grooves. Go to 4.

4. a. Length to 85 feet; up to 88 throat grooves reaching to umbilicus; dorsal fin less than 12 inches high, set far back on body; light gray-blue with lighter mottling on belly, sides, and back; up to 395 wide black baleen plates per side, each up to 3 feet long with up to 75 bristles per inch. BLUE WHALE.

   b. Length to 79 feet; up to 100 throat grooves reaching to umbilicus; prominent dorsal fin up to 24 inches high; lower-right lip and sometimes upper-right lip white; up to 473 baleen plates per side, each up to 2.5 feet long with up to 88 bristles per inch; anterior 100 or so baleen plates on right side only are light, remaining plates are dark. FINBACK WHALE.

   c. Length to 62 feet; dark body but may have oval white spots on sides; up to 56 throat grooves reaching only slightly past flipper, not to umbilicus; up to 340 dark baleen plates per side, each up to 2.5 feet long with up to 150 fine white bristles per inch. SEI WHALE.

B. Toothed Whales (Odontocetes)

5. a. Length to 60 feet (males) or 38 feet (females); massive square head with blowhole at left tip; narrow lower jaw with up to 25 large teeth in each side; dorsal hump; triangular flukes with deep central notch; wrinkled skin. SPERM WHALE.
   b. Length under 30 feet. Go to 6.
6. a. Dorsal fin present. Go to 7.
   b. No dorsal fin; length to 16 feet; body all white (juveniles gray or brown); 8–10 pairs of teeth in each jaw, up to 2/3 inch diameter. BELUGA.
   c. No dorsal fin; length to 16 feet; body gray or blotched white on gray; one (rarely both) upper incisor extends as long tusk; no other teeth; arctic only. NARWHAL.
7. a. Jaws of whole animal not drawn out into beak. Go to 8.
   b. Jaws of whole animal extended forward as distinct beak. Go to 11.
   c. If skull is found, see 9 and 10 before continuing to 11.
8. a. Small dorsal fin. Go to 9.
   b. Large dorsal fin. Go to 10.
9. a. Length to 5 feet; up to 30 pairs of small, flattened, spade-shaped teeth in each jaw; small triangular dorsal fin, often with small, rough, wartlike growths on leading edge. HARBOR PORPOISE.
   b. Length to 11 feet; sharklike snout; jaw like sperm whale's with 12–16 pairs of sharp, recurved teeth, lower jaw only; upper jaw toothless. PYGMY SPERM WHALE.
10. a. Length to 30 feet; dorsal fin up to 6 feet high; body black above with white patch behind eye, gray saddle behind dorsal fin, and white of belly extending up on sides; 10–12 pairs of teeth in each jaw, up to 1 or 2 inches diameter. KILLER WHALE.
    b. Length to 20 feet; rounded forehead overhangs short snout; very long-based, curved, round-tipped dorsal fin set well forward of midbody; curved and pointed flippers; jet black except for anchor-shaped gray patch

on chest; 8–10 pairs of teeth in upper and lower jaws, 1/2 inch diameter. PILOT WHALE, POTHEAD.

c. Lenth to 14 feet; gray body, with many white scratches or scars; blunt snout; usually 3–7 teeth, 1/2 inch diameter on each side of lower jaw, usually none in upper; curved, pointed dorsal fin up to 15 inches high is usually darker than body. GRAY GRAMPUS.

11. a. Distinct black-and-white color pattern and/or many teeth in both jaws. Go to 12.

b. Basically uniform color, usually dark gray, black, or brownish; 2–4 teeth in lower jaw only; 2 throat grooves join to form forward-pointing V; flukes without central notch; small triangular dorsal fin. Go to 13.

12. a. Length to 10 feet; body dark above, light below, white patch on side runs aft from below dorsal fin and sweeps over the ridge of back; short snout usually white, rarely black; 22–28 teeth on each side of upper and lower jaws, 1/4 inch diameter. WHITE-BEAKED DOLPHIN.

b. Length to 9 feet; body dark above, white on belly, white patch on side runs aft from below dorsal fin but does not reach over ridge of back; yellow or tan streak behind white patch; short, dark snout; 30–40 teeth on each side of upper and lower jaws, 3/16 inch diameter. WHITE-SIDED DOLPHIN.

c. Length to 8 feet; dark above, white below, with gray or yellowish crisscross or figure-eight pattern on sides; 40–50 teeth on each side of upper and lower jaws, 1/10 inch diameter. COMMON DOLPHIN.

d. Length to 9 feet; body dark above, with white of belly sweeping up over eye and flipper toward dorsal fin and ridge of black; distinct dark line from eye along lower side to anus; 43–50 teeth on each side of upper and lower jaws, 1/8 inch diameter. STRIPED DOLPHIN.

e. Length to 12 feet; body gray above, lighter on belly; dark stripes run from base of short beak to eye and blowholes; no distinct color pattern; 22–26 teeth on each side of upper and lower jaws, 1/8 inch diameter. BOTTLENOSE DOLPHIN.

13. a. Length to 30 feet; color gray to light brown or yellowish; large forehead bulges over short beak; two small teeth at tip of lower jaw; light gray indentation between head and rest of body; relatively small curved dorsal fin located behind midpoint of body. NORTHERN BOTTLENOSE WHALE.
    b. Length to 17 feet; black above, gray on belly; small dorsal fin located toward rear of body; 2 small flattened teeth at tip of lower jaw. TRUE'S BEAKED WHALE.
    c. Length to 15 feet; body all dark; one large tooth (up to 6 inches, only tip exposed) in massive triangular prominence midway along lower jaw; small triangular dorsal fin located just behind midbody; flukes lack central notch. DENSE-BEAKED WHALE.
    d. Length to 16 feet; body dark; one flattened tooth located midway along each side of lower jaw, tip directed posteriorly; small dorsal fin; flukes lack central notch. NORTH SEA BEAKED WHALE.

FORM 80-1

GULF OF MAINE
Whale Sighting Network

Fold and mail to: **ALLIED WHALE** College of the Atlantic Bar Harbor, Maine 04609 (207) 288-5644 or 5015

Your name _____ Address _____ Zip _____ Phone _____

INSTRUCTIONS: Please complete this form and CIRCLE ON THE ILLUSTRATIONS ANY FEATURE THAT YOU OBSERVED. Photograph animals if possible, especially undersides of humpback flukes. Space is provided for you to sketch any unusual markings or tags or to draw species not illustrated.

Date _____, 19 _____ Time _____ am/pm. Weather and sea conditions _____ Temp. _____

Nearest land mark _____ Lat./long, Loran _____ Depth _____

Type of whale or porpoise sighted _____ Size _____ Number _____ Photographs? _____

How far were you from the animals? _____ Which direction were they swimming? _____ In a tight school? _____

The whale spouted ____ times, with ____ seconds between spouts. Then it dived for ____ minutes before spouting again. _____

Describe the animal's behavior (feeding, jumping, tail raised in air, etc.) _____

Describe any fishes, birds, or other marine life seen near the whales or porpoises. _____

FOLD HERE

COMMONLY SEEN:

finback whale 30-70 ft.

right side of jaws light, left dark

FOLD HERE

humpback whale 30-55 ft.

bumps on snout

15 ft. rough edges

flukes often raised when diving

photographs can identify individuals

white flipper-15 ft. long

minke whale 15-25 ft.

pointed snout often breaks surface

light gray sweeps up from chest

white patch on flipper

FOLD HERE

right whale 30-55 ft.

rough white patches

V-spout

12 ft. smooth edges

flukes often raised when diving

no dorsal fin

dark undersides

harbor porpoise 4-6 ft.

pothead or pilot whale 10-20 ft.

long based fin

bulbous head

FOLD HERE

OCCASIONALLY SEEN:

saddleback dolphin 6-8 ft.

criss cross pattern on side

killer whale 15-25 ft.

male fin, 5 ft. — female fin, 3 ft.

gray

white patch

white sided dolphin 7-9 ft.

tan

white

white beaked dolphin 8-10 ft.

white back

white

D.D. Tyler

BONUSES *for* WHALE WATCHERS: BASKING SHARKS, SUNFISH, *and* LEATHERBACK TURTLES

During the past ten years we have received from whale watchers and fishermen many reports of basking sharks, ocean sunfish, and leatherback turtles. Most people are surprised to learn that these animals are regular summer visitors to our study area. These sightings generate so many intriguing considerations that we have included brief species accounts.

Species Accounts

BASKING SHARK
(Cetorhinus maximus)

Basking Shark
size range: up to 45 feet
Sarah Landry

This huge fish, which can be up to 45 feet (13.7 m) long, is second in size only to the whale shark and is frequently seen during summer in our study area by whale watchers and fishermen. These sharks demonstrate a remarkable evolutionary convergence on the feeding method of baleen whales, for both strain planktonic animals from the water.

Basking sharks occur throughout the temperate and boreal waters of the North Atlantic, from Newfoundland to North Carolina, and from Norway to the Mediterranean. Within our study area they are most common during late July or August in the southern part of the Gulf of Maine and in the Gulf of St. Lawrence, but they are also well known in Newfoundland. They are found singly or in groups of up to ten or more. We have seen groups of six or eight, head to tail, slowly swimming in a circle. Other observers have also reported this unexplained behavior.

The best features for identification at sea are large size —most specimens are from 12 to 30 feet (3.7–9.1 m) long— and the large, floppy, triangular dorsal fin. Furthermore, the caudal fin often breaks the surface as the shark moves sluggishly along. These animals are very docile, almost completely harmless, and can be approached closely. Their teeth are minute. At close range the five large gill openings can be seen encircling the neck. Each of these openings contains a gill arch , and each arch is adorned with many horny, bristle-like gill rakers. The gill rakers look like baleen (whalebone), and fishermen or whalermen in times past therefore called these animals "bone sharks." The scientific name also recognizes this similarity, translating roughly as "big whale-nosed" shark. As the shark swims lazily along with its large mouth open, water streams through the gill openings and the rakers strain out copepods and other small animals. Periodically the shark must close the gill openings and "backflush" the collected plankton into the throat for swallowing. *Calanus finmarchicus* is the main food from spring through autumn. Nobody knows what these animals do in winter, although it may be that they shed their gill rakers, remain inactive on the bottom, then grow new rakers for resumption of feeding in spring.

Basking sharks have been hunted with harpoons throughout their range, because the enormous liver, which constitutes up to 25 percent of the body weight, is a rich source of oil. A liver can yield between 80 and 600 gallons (300–2,260 liters) of oil, which was used for burning in lamps before the discovery of petroleum. Early hunting by

Basking shark harpooned off Pemaquid Point, Maine, July 7, 1968. Weight 1,850 pounds (839 kg). Note gill slits extending almost completely around head. Everett Boutilier

American colonists during the first half of the 1700s and thereafter may have reduced the abundance of this species in the Gulf of Maine to this day. Sperm whalers out of New Bedford also hunted it, because its oil was about as good as sperm oil for lighting purposes. Despite the lazy, inoffensive nature of this shark when undisturbed, harpooned specimens proved to be feisty and strong. There still is a small commercial market for basking sharks, but unfortunately some animals are killed for sport, and others die accidentally from entanglement in fishing gear.

It can be seen that basking sharks exhibit several interesting parallels with right whales. Their warm-season distributions are the same; they eat the same food and catch it in the same way; and both may have suffered a long-lasting population decline as a result of early overhunting. Furthermore, both of these huge, bizarre-looking animals often form the basis of "sea monster" stories. We welcome reports of basking shark sightings in the hopes that such data might be useful for detecting population trends and for comparison with future sightings of right whales.

OCEAN SUNFISH
(Mola mola)

Ocean Sunfish
size: 8 to 11 feet or more
Sarah Landry

As a result of its large size and strange appearance, the ocean sunfish regularly generates more puzzled inquiries than any other large fish in our study area. This fish can grow to at least 11 feet (3.4 m) long and 2,000 pounds (907 kg). The oval body with its large eye and tall, swordlike dorsal and anal fins completely lacks a caudal fin. A person seeing his first ocean sunfish, especially a big one, could be excused for thinking he saw a small whale whose tail had been chopped off. More than one caller has made such a description to us. The animal is called a sunfish because it is often seen lazing at the surface on a sunny day. At such times it usually lies on its side or tips slowly back and forth, the tall dorsal fin waving in the air. Other local names, such as "moonfish" or "headfish," refer to the somewhat circular body and the lack of distinction between head and body.

Ocean sunfish are summer visitors to coastal waters throughout our study area. They are regularly seen during July and August in the Gulf of Maine, especially southern sections; along the outer Nova Scotia coast; in the Gulf of St. Lawrence; and on the Newfoundland Banks. We would expect to receive twenty or forty reports of ocean sunfish each year in the Gulf of Maine, and many more animals probably go unreported.

Surprisingly little is known about this species, and some of the things that are known are equally surprising. The sunfish is found worldwide in tropical and temperate seas. The individuals that enter our continental shelf waters certainly come from warmer offshore waters. The listless attitude of the ocean sunfish when seen in our study area has suggested to most previous observers that the fish cannot long survive our cold waters and will surely die by winter, at the latest. While this may be true, it is worthwhile to consider the possibility that the sunfish are in less distress than has been suggested, and several observations may be cited in support of this idea. First, although sunfish in our waters are passive enough to be approached easily, fishermen who have harpooned them have been startled by their vigorous resistance to being taken. Obviously the fish have a good deal of power in reserve. Second, plenty of food for these fish exists in our waters, and they are able to catch it. The sunfish's diet apparently consists largely of jellyfish, comb jellies (ctenophores), and salps, plus some other, harder invertebrates. Exactly how a fish can get to be so big feeding on such watery, unnutritious fare is something of a mystery, but the summer waters of our study area provide a rich supply of a

Ocean sunfish. Carl Haycock

Ocean sunfish, caught in lobster trap lines near Isleford, Maine, by David Layton on July 20, 1982, and photographed at the J. S. Humphreys Wharf, Southwest Harbor, Maine. Approximate weight 400 pounds (181 kg). Steven Katona

number of these jellies, and we have obtained the remains of the common lion's mane jellyfish, *Cyanea arctica*, from a harpooned specimen. We have also watched a dying sunfish defecate a rusty red liquid that matched the color of that jellyfish. We hope someday to tag some of these curious fish to see whether any might survive their forays into the study area.

Despite the potential giant size of this species, the average size is about 3 to 5 feet (91–152 cm) long and 175 to 500 pounds (79–227 kg). We dissected a harpooned specimen that weighed 575 pounds (260 kg). The skin was exceptionally thick and tough, was covered with rough, sharklike denticles, and could be cut only with great difficulty. The entire skeleton was cartilaginous, like a shark's, even though this is a teleost (bony) fish. The skin and gills carried several dozen parasitic copepods and other crustaceans. We boiled up the fins in hopes of making a mock shark's fin soup, but the result was poor. We had better luck with the abundant meat, which proved to be thick and fleshy, more like chicken than fish, and quite tasty when stir-fried. Several years later we saw the ocean sunfish included in a compendium of poisonous ocean creatures, apparently because its family (Molidae) is related to the family of fishes (Tetraodontiformidae) that includes puffers, whose gonads are deadly poisonous. We have not been able to discover what parts of its body, if any, are actually poisonous.

Ocean sunfish, close-up of sharklike skin. Steven Katona

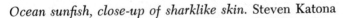

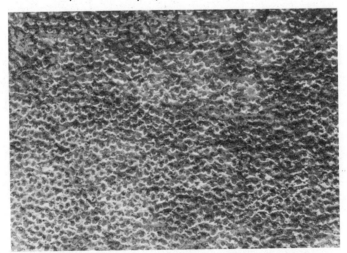

LEATHERBACK TURTLE
(Dermochelys coriacea)

Leatherback Turtle
size: 6 to 11 feet or more
Sarah Landry

Whale watchers and fishermen in our study area may see the world's heaviest reptile, the leatherback turtle, which is known to grow to a maximum size of at least 11 feet (3.4) m) long and 1,900 pounds (862 kg). Turtles are a far cry from whales and seals, but we include the leatherback in the hope that sightings contributed by readers of this guide will add an an understanding of this endangered species and ultimately aid its survival.

Identification of this species is easy. It is the only turtle in the world with 5 to 7 ridges that run the full length of the shell. The leathery shell itself is made of thousands of nearly indistinguishably tiny bones, and doesn't look at all like a normal turtle shell. The leatherback's extremely long front flippers are also distinctive. Leatherbacks in our study area are usually mature and frequently measure over 6 feet (1.8 m) in length and weigh over 1,000 pounds (454 kg). They are seen singly in our area, although loose aggregations have occasionally been reported from southeastern or Gulf Coast states.

The leatherback, found in all oceans except the Antarctic, is a regular summer visitor to waters around Cape Cod, the Gulf of Maine, and Nova Scotia. It is found occasionally in Newfoundland. It is the only marine turtle that has been able to colonize cold waters for feeding and the only species that regularly occurs in the open waters of our study area.

Why do leatherbacks come here? They come to feed on jellyfish, especially the lion's mane jellyfish (which itself may reach 6 feet, or 1.8 m, in diameter), and on comb jellies, salps, or other jelly organisms that are numerous in our waters during summer. The mouth, throat, and esophagus are lined with numerous spines up to 2 inches (5 cm) long that point inward, presumably to aid in swallowing long, slippery jellyfish. The similarity of the diet of leatherbacks and ocean sunfish suggests that observers ought to expect the two species to occur in the same area. Individuals are known to remain in our waters for at least several weeks.

How do leatherbacks survive in these cold waters? The surprising answer is that they are warm-blooded. All four flippers contain countercurrent heat-exchange systems. Arteries carrying blood to the flippers are surrounded by veins returning blood to the body. The arterial blood gives up its heat, but not its oxygen or nutrients, to the venous blood. Metabolic heat is thus retained in the massive body, to the extent that leatherbacks in 45°F (7.2°C) water can maintain a body temperature of about 80°F (27°C). This is ex-

Leatherback turtle, caught accidentally in lobster fishing gear near Round Pond, Maine, August 1, 1979. This turtle was nearly 7 feet (213 cm) long and 1,500 pounds (680 kg). Ventral view, showing long flippers. Everett Boutilier

actly the same anatomical adaptation found in cetacean (or pinniped) flippers, flukes, and dorsal fins for heat conservation.

Where do our leatherbacks come from? Western North Atlantic leatherbacks breed from April to November, mainly on a few beaches in Central or South America, although occasional females nest as far north as southern Florida. Leatherbacks appear to wander or migrate farther than any other marine turtle, and their 2,000-mile (3,200-km) swim to eat jellyfish in our study area is not unusual for the species. Females may nest only every other year, during March and April, and may not migrate as far north during breeding years. Perhaps this accounts for the preponderance of males among specimens recorded from our waters.

What is the fate of leatherbacks that visit our study area? Most of the turtles probably go offshore and south again in autumn. Until recently, leatherbacks that were seen were often shot or harpooned, mainly out of curiosity. Since the meat is not edible and there is no shell, there has never been any other reason to kill a leatherback. Fortunately, this uniquely interesting turtle is now protected by the Endangered Species Act of 1973. However, some of the turtles get into difficulty of their own accord, for about one-third of all specimens recorded from our waters were found entangled in lobster fishing gear. One clever theory put forth to explain those entanglements holds that the turtles on occasion mistake a lobster pot buoy for a jellyfish. The pot buoy, floating at the surface and covered with algal fuzz, might indeed attract a turtle, whose long flippers might then get caught in the line running to the trap. If the lobsterman finds the turtle in time, it can be released unharmed; however, the animal's struggles may entangle it so tightly or the efforts of dragging the traps around may exhaust it so much that it drowns before being found.

Marine turtles and marine mammals are eons apart in their evolutionary history, yet the leatherback shares many characteristics with a big whale such as a humpback. Both are large, long-distance travelers of the world's oceans, with long lifetimes, regular migration cycles, and similar adapta-

Dorsal view of leatherback turtle caught in lobster gear near Corea, Maine, showing longitudinal ridges. Katherine Heidiger

tions for staying warm in cold water. Both reproduce in specific breeding locations, and both are now on the Endangered Species List. An actual ecological relationship between a leatherback and any of our marine mammals is practically nonexistent, but their similarities are independently evolved adaptations to solve shared environmental challenges. Perhaps the most critical factor shared by leatherbacks (and all marine turtles) and marine mammals is their dependence on human respect and restraint for their future survival.

Part Three

SEALS

Harbor seal pup reared at College of the Atlantic, showing the ear opening. The light spot on the head is white paint applied at release to facilitate reidentification. Steve Donoso

Introduction

THE ONLY OTHER TRULY MARINE MAMMALS FOUND IN OUR PART
of the North Atlantic Ocean besides cetaceans are the seals.
We are too far south for polar bears, too far north for manatees, and sea otters never colonized this ocean. Although salt
water may be a temporary habitat for certain other mammals of our region—for example, white-tailed deer (*Odo-
coileus virginianus*), moose (*Alces alces*), and beaver (*Cas-
tor canadensis*)—they take to nearshore waters only when
swimming to an island or when pursued by predators or
hunters. Island-dwelling otters (*Lutra canadensis*) or minks
(*Mustela vison*) may regularly forage for fish or other prey
in salt water during some seasons. The maritime habit was
even better developed in the extinct sea mink (*Mustela ma-
crodon*), a fat, generally reddish fur-bearer that ranged in
size from about 20 to 33 inches (51–84 cm), nose to tip of
tail, and lived along the rocky shores of Maine and the Bay
of Fundy. Sea minks were extirpated by overhunting before
their behavior was recorded, but we must assume they repro-
duced on land, wintered ashore, and had limited endurance

Harbor seal resting at Mt. Desert Rock, Maine, showing V-shaped nostrils and five long nails on each foreflipper. Bob Mackenzie

in the ocean. The last known specimen was taken at Campobello Island, New Brunswick, in 1894, nine years before the sea mink was formally described by a scientist and recognized as a distinct species.

Seals and humans have for centuries shared a mutual curiosity. Seals often surface very near to boats, stare with their inquisitive globular eyes, and then suddenly dive with an exuberant slap of their powerful rear flippers. For humans, however, seals have not been merely the object of study for the curious naturalist or scientist. For thousands of years seals have been hunted in the arctic to provide life's essentials for natives and their dogs: meat; oil for light and heat; hides for boots, clothing, and skin boat covering; and strong rawhide thongs for harnesses, lashings, and tools. However, the insatiable desire of American and European markets for furs made sealskins an important trading item. Small-scale commercial sealing of the immense herds in the Canadian arctic began in the seventh century. By the early nineteenth century, seal harvesting was recognized as a lucrative industry, and it compensated for the declining bowhead whale and sperm whale fisheries. Subsequently, intense hunting of harp, hooded, bearded, and ringed seals and of walruses has severely reduced stocks and caused us to realize that the survival of these species will depend on good management and protection efforts. Recent public awareness has stimulated population studies and scientific investigations to learn more about all aspects of seal biology.

All the fur seals, sea lions, walruses, and true seals belong to the order of mammals called Pinnipedia (from the Latin meaning wing- or feather-footed). Within this order, fur seals and sea lions belong to the family Otariidae, and true seals to the family Phocidae. These two families evolved quite separately and show several differences in their anatomy and adaptations to terrestrial and aquatic locomotion. Walruses (family Odobenidae), which may have evolved from an early branch of the otariid line, are unique but display similarities to both otariid and phocid groups.

The three families can be summarized as follows: the fur seals and sea lions (Otariidae), which probably had a bearlike ancestor, are characterized by visible ear pinnae and long, sinuous necks; foreflippers which are long and almost hairless, with thin webbing and rudimentary claws; and long, webbed, almost hairless hindflippers which can be turned forward for movement on land. The hindflipper claws are rudimentary on the outer two digits, but well developed on the middle three digits. The testes are contained in a scrotum, and the tail is distinct and free from the body. Propulsion in the water is accomplished by simultaneous penguinlike strokes of the foreflippers, while movement on land is achieved by running or walking with the body supported on all four limbs.

The true seals (also called "hair seals" or "earless seals") are all classified in the family Phocidae and are thought to have evolved from an otterlike ancestor. Ear pinnae are lacking, and there is no clearly defined neck region. The foreflippers are short and haired, with digits united in thick tissue; each digit terminates in a prominent claw. The hind-flippers are of intermediate length, haired, with extensive thin webbing, and claws on all five digits. The hindflippers are directed backward and cannot be turned forward. Testes are internal, and the tail is distinct and free from the body. These seals swim by lateral flexion of the posterior part of the body and side-to-side sculling of the webbed hindflip-pers. Movement on land is rather clumsy even though it can be quick. The seal crawls by hitching the front flippers for-ward, then humping the body like an inchworm to advance the hindquarters. The drawings below will help the reader visualize differences between seals and sea lions.

Seal

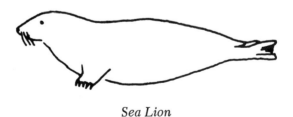

Sea Lion

The walruses (Odobenidae) have no ear pinnae, and the ear canal is covered by a fold of skin. They have a thick, robust, sparsely haired to nearly hairless body. The fore-flippers, similar to those of sea lions but relatively shorter, are sparsely haired, with five small, distinct claws. The hind-flippers, too, resemble those of sea lions. They are sparsely haired, webbed, and can be turned forward; claws are rudimentary on the outer two digits, but well developed on the middle three digits. Testes are internal, and the tail is enclosed in a web of skin. Walruses have highly specialized dentition with very long upper canines. Their locomotion in water involves sea lion-like foreflipper strokes and seallike sweeps of the hindflippers. On land they walk or run supported on all four limbs.

The North Atlantic is unique among the world's oceans in having no otariid pinnipeds, so there will be no further discussion of them except to note that California sea lions (*Zalophus californianus*) that have escaped from captivity very occasionally appear off the East Coast of North America. One was killed in Newfoundland in 1965.

Seals have a streamlined, torpedolike form, with reduced forelimbs that can be flattened against the body, and hindlimbs modified for swimming. Genitalia and mammaries lie beneath the body's smooth surface. The skin has a thick, tough epidermis rich with blood vessels and covered by flattened hairs well supplied with oil glands. Under the skin lies a layer of blubber, which provides insulation against cold, a source of reserve energy, buoyancy, and padding to enhance the streamlined body shape.

Seals breathe air like other mammals, yet display remarkable diving capabilities, submerging for periods lasting from 5 to 40 minutes and, in some species, descending to 200 fathoms or more. To withstand pressures at depth, the seal empties its lungs before diving, and depends on oxygen stored by the hemoglobin of the blood and the myoglobin of the muscles. During a dive, circulation to most of the body is drastically curtailed, except to the brain and vital internal organs. In addition, heartbeat slows to as low as one-tenth

the normal rate, and body temperature and metabolic rate are reduced to conserve oxygen. A seal may attain a swimming speed of up to 8 miles (13 km) per hour, but the bulky, less-streamlined walrus is slower.

Pinnipeds are carnivores. Their diet generally consists of fish and invertebrates, but does not exclude birds or mammals; the antarctic leopard seal, for example, is partial to penguins and crabeater seal pups, and our local gray seal occasionally supplements its fish regimen with ducks or black guillemots. Like other carnivorous mammals, pinnipeds are intelligent and have well-developed senses. Vision is keen in water, functional in air, and somewhat adaptable to the darkness of ocean depths and the long winter's night of high latitudes. Nevertheless, sight is not essential for survival, as shown by numerous reports of blind though otherwise healthy seals in the wild.

Although our knowledge of a seal's sensory world is imperfect, some generalizations can be made. Hearing is acute in both air and water. The seal's ear, a short distance behind the eye, appears externally as a small wrinkle and an aperture that is open in air and closed during dives. The internal ear bones are massive compared with those of terrestrial mammals. With their vocal cords, seals produce diverse species-specific vocalizations in air and water, and certain

Harbor seals on a half-tide ledge. Flanders Bay, Maine, July 1982. Steven Katona

clicking sounds have been detected that seem to some investigators suitable for echolocation. Nevertheless, years of research have thus far failed to produce convincing evidence for pinniped echolocation. The tactile sense is important. Vibrissae, or whiskers, are coarse, continuously growing, nerve-equipped hairs located above the eyes and on lateral pads of the upper lips. These whiskers are sensitive to vibration and touch and apparently play a role in food capture at short range. The olfactory sense operates both in air—as when a cow seal identifies her hauled-out pup by its smell—and underwater via the rhinarium, which surrounds the nostrils and is similar to a dog's wet nose, picking up stimuli from dissolved molecules. As is the case with the ear, nostrils are normally closed and are opened by voluntary muscles only when the head is above water.

Little is known of feeding and other behavior at sea. Seals are most conspicuous when hauled out to rest, breed, or molt, on rocks, sand, or ice, usually where an adjacent channel or other steep dropoff allows for rapid access to the water. Many species are highly gregarious, and haulouts of hundreds or even thousands of individuals are not uncommon, particularly at the time of molting. Seals on shore are wary and easily frightened into the sea, but a cautious approach terminating several hundred feet from a haulout site will permit satisfactory viewing with binoculars or telescope. Bear in mind that seals which haul out on land (i.e., gray and harbor seals) generally do so during low tide hours, except on salt marsh banks, where high tide haulout may occur. Seal watching can reward the curious naturalist with a list of questions, many of which have not yet been answered. There are other benefits, too, for a quiet session of observation, punctuated only by the cries of gulls and the muffled barking of seals across the water, can restore one's sense of time, patience, and well-being.

Though seals in the water are often less noticeable than they are on land, they can be seen at times resting, feeding, and even leaping, rolling, and splashing. In their watery element seals (especially the young) may be bold and curious and come close to boats or shorelines to stare at humans and their dogs. However, any sudden movements may frighten the seals, which loudly smack their flippers on the water surface and rush away to a safe distance before reappearing.

Details of reproductive behavior are given in the species accounts. In most seals, whelping (giving birth) takes place on land or ice, followed within a few weeks by mating. The new embryo does not grow for several months, a phenomenon known as delayed implantation; the start of fetal development is so timed that gestation takes about one year. Because of this important adaptation pups are born at the most favorable season, and the behavior of breeding adults is synchronized.

Seal watchers in our study area are fortunate because this region contains or may be visited by five of the six true seals found in the North Atlantic. Coastal islands, sandbars, and ledges from Cape Cod to Labrador are inhabited seasonally or all year by up to thousands of harbor and gray seals. Sea ice in the Gulf of St. Lawrence and offshore from Newfoundland is used for pupping and mating by many thousands of harp and hooded seals. It is obvious that these energetic predators, each of which may consume up to 10 percent of its body weight in fish per day, play an important part in the ecology of the waters they frequent. The ringed seal, while abundant and ecologically important in the arctic,

Gray seal pup and female. Sable Island, Nova Scotia. Geoff Beck

is only a rare visitor to the northern portion of our study area. The sixth phocid seal known from the Atlantic is the bearded seal (*Erignathus barbatus*), an arctic species that does not now reach our area. It is large, up to 7.5 feet (2.3 m) long and 750 pounds (336 kg), with long vibrissae, prominent brow ridges, and "square" flippers, so called because all five digits on the foreflipper are of equal length, whereas in other seals the digits decrease in length from first to last. The rather solitary "square flipper" frequents shallow arctic seas and moving ice floes, diving for shellfish, other invertebrates, and polar cod. This is the seal used by Eskimos for mukluks and skin boats. Little is known of its biology. Bones of bearded seals dating from the most recent glaciation have been dredged up in the Gulf of Maine, suggesting that this species extended its range as its habitat expanded, then retreated as the ice receded. Finally, the walrus is now rare south of northern Labrador and Greenland, although it frequented the Gulf of St. Lawrence and Sable Island in historic times.

In addition to their roles in natural ecosystems, pinnipeds play an important part in human economies wherever they occur abundantly. The high productivity of shallow arctic seas can support enormous stocks of walrus and several species of seals, if humans do not deplete the fisheries or pollute the ocean. Walruses and all arctic seals are still vitally important to subsistence of local natives who hunt them for

177

Gray seal (left) and harbor seal (right), showing great size difference. Little Duck Island, Maine. Bob Bowman

food, oil, fur, and hides. Norway and Canada annually conduct a large commercial harvest of harp and hooded seals, for their pelts, off Newfoundland and Labrador. Gray and harbor seals have little direct commercial value despite their substantial numbers. In fact, they have been bountied in both the Gulf of Maine and eastern Canada at various times because of suspected competition with fishermen, damage to fishery gear, or involvement in the life cycle of parasites of commercial fishes. In U.S. waters all pinnipeds are protected by the Marine Mammal Protection Act of 1972.

Pinnipeds wherever they occur are clearly of interest and importance to humans, but our knowledge of them is limited, despite many scientific studies completed or in progress. The amateur observer can make valuable contributions to our understanding of seals by keeping careful records. Sighting data and forms for submission of census are provided on pages 210–13. Be on the lookout for brands and hindflipper tags, as seals of some species have been individually marked in order to track their movements. We look forward to your reports. Several commercial natural history cruises that provide opportunities to observe seals are listed in Appendix II. References on seals of our study area are in the Bibliography. We highly recommend A. W. Mansfield's *Seals of Arctic and Eastern Canada.*

Species Accounts

Length is measured in a straight line from nose to tip of tail.

HARBOR SEAL
(Phoca vitulina concolor)

Harbor seal cow nursing pup, with typical seal ledge in background.
size range: up to 6 feet
D. D. Tyler

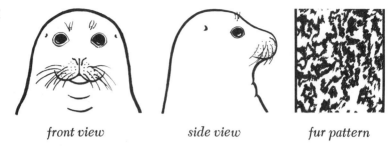

Harbor Seal
D. D. Tyler

front view   *side view*   *fur pattern*

In New England this is by far the commonest and most frequently reported seal; it is relatively rarer, but still familiar, in eastern Canada. These two regions lie in the center of the species' northwest Atlantic distribution.

Harbor seals bask and sleep on coastal islands, ledges, and sandbars during low tide and forage during high tide, although high tide haulout may occur on salt marsh banks. In water the seals may be bold and curious about human activity. The young in particular often surface next to boats, staring inquisitively.

The scientific name (Gr. *phoca*, seal, + L. *vitulus*, calf) means "sea calf" or, more loosely, "sea dog." Indeed, the harbor seal head viewed in profile reveals a short muzzle and a concave forehead like that of a cocker spaniel. The eye is roughly equidistant from tip of nose to ear opening, and in

Harbor seal ripping mackerel apart. D. D. Tyler

a frontal view the nostrils form a broad V, almost meeting at the bottom. Pelage (coat) color varies from light gray or tan to brown, black, or even reddish, with fine dark mottling or spotting on the back, becoming more scattered on the belly. A complete spectrum of these pelages can often be observed within a group of several dozen basking seals.

Adult males average 5 feet (153 cm) and 200 pounds (90 kg) and may attain 5 feet 6 inches (168 cm) and 250 pounds (112 kg). Adult females average 4 feet 8 inches (143 cm) and 156 pounds (70 kg) and may reach 5 feet 6 inches (168 cm) and 200 pounds (90 kg). Males mature at 4 to 6 years of age and females at 3 to 4 years. The sexes are very similar, not only in size but also in pelage color and pattern and in head features, so they are difficult to tell apart in the wild except when the bellies are seen. The configurations illustrated below apply to all North Atlantic seals except bearded seals, and walruses.

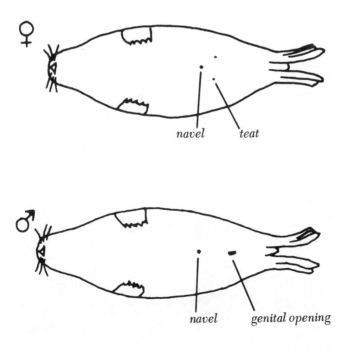

navel   teat

navel   genital opening

Young harbor seal, showing concave, doglike head profile. Christopher Packard

Gray seal head, showing long straight nose and W shape of nostrils. Christopher Packard

The harbor seal is widely distributed in nearshore waters of all northern oceans and their adjoining seas above about 30° north latitude. Bays, estuaries, and even some accessible lakes are occupied if certain features are present, including islets, reefs, or shoals; sheltered inlets; and freedom from human interference. The present breeding range in the northwest Atlantic extends from ice-free waters of the Arctic to New Hampshire, though there is evidence that breeding occurred as far south as Cape Cod Bay in the first half of the twentieth century. Harbor seals regularly winter south to Long Island, New York, and occasionally to the Carolinas, rarely appearing in Florida.

In the last century harbor seals inhabited Lake Ontario and Lake Champlain, having gained entry via the St. Law-

Harbor seal, close-up of foreflipper, showing five stout nails. Steven Katona

rence River, but today they seldom reach Montreal. In eastern Canada the seals occur in the St. Lawrence estuary and Northumberland Strait; at Anticosti, the Magdalen Islands, and Newfoundland; and in greatest numbers along the shores of Nova Scotia, including Sable Island. They are found also near Grand Manan Island in the Bay of Fundy. In 1973 the eastern Canada population (south of Labrador) was 12,700 and declining; it is now thought to be expanding, but no exact figures are available yet.

Harbor seals in eastern Canada are found in generally small, probably isolated populations, most of which have not been studied in detail. More information is available for the New England population, which from spring through autumn is spread along the Maine and New Hampshire coast in several hundred colonies, the largest ones containing up to 150 or more seals. The greatest concentration of seals is in Machias and Penobscot bays, and off Mt. Desert and Swans islands. Aerial surveys over the past few years show that the Maine population is increasing and is now 12,000 to 15,000. Although some harbor seals overwinter in northern New England, by the end of November Maine populations diminish and hundreds of seals start to appear around Cape Cod and southward to Long Island. The winter migration evidently reverses in the following spring, and by early May Maine's seal herds are almost back to normal size, while counts in southern New England dwindle, approaching zero by early June.

In late spring, pregnant females move to upper reaches of bays and estuaries and seek out protected areas on reefs or islands, somewhat apart from males and juveniles. Pups are born from late April to mid-June, weighing 21 pounds (9.5 kg) and measuring 2.5 feet (76 cm) on average. Usually the natal coat is like that of the adult, but up to 25 percent of the pups at some Canadian colonies are born with long white fur called lanugo (from Latin for "downy"). This is always shed by 2 weeks of age and replaced with the adult type of coat. Pups can and do swim shortly after birth. Nursing takes place ashore or in the water and lasts about 30 days.

Harbor seal, showing V-shaped nostrils. The long vibrissae of the eyebrows and mustache are visible. Mt. Desert Rock, Maine. Steven Mullane

The first-year mortality rate is about 30 percent; some of the causes are storms, abandonment by the mother, disease, parasites, and predation by sharks and possibly even killer whales. Annual mortality in subsequent years is about 13 percent. Harbor seals have lived to 35 years in captivity, but natural longevity may be slightly lower.

Mating occurs from early May to August, invariably in the water. This aspect of behavior is poorly understood. Seals may be seen chasing each other and rolling and splashing in pairs or trios during the mating season, but also in most other months. The appearance of cuts and scars on some mature males at this season suggests that there is competition for females.

Molting takes place in July and August. Just prior to the molt, the hair, when dry, becomes dull brown and the pattern indistinct. The new coat usually appears pale and silvery when dry. In late summer some harbor seals move offshore to deeper water, presumably to feed.

Harbor seals eat fish and invertebrates as available; the most common food items are herring, squid, alewife, flounder, and hake.

During the late 1800s, Maine and Massachusetts offered a one-dollar bounty on harbor seals in order to reduce the population and perhaps increase the amount of fish caught by humans. By the early 1900s Maine's harbor seals were nearly exterminated in certain localities, with no noticeable effect on fish catches, but the seals made a good comeback after the Maine bounty was lifted in 1905. Massachusetts meanwhile retained the bounty until 1962, and this may have led to the extirpation of breeding activity in Cape Cod Bay.

Increased human use of the coast in eastern Canada has disturbed harbor seals and driven them to occupy more exposed breeding sites, with greater danger to their pups. This and bounty hunting may have contributed to population decline in that region up to 1976, when the bounty ended. Now the trend is reversed, and eastern Canadian stocks are increasing rapidly, according to one Canadian scientist.

Of all the seals in our area, harbor seals are the most highly adapted to water. Their visible surface behavior ranges from dozing to inquisitiveness to playful leaping and porpoising, but the details of their underwater activities remain unknown. Despite the commonness of this seal in our study area, many questions remain, and a satisfactory understanding of this attractive and appealing animal will require further observation and research.

Harbor seal, close-up of hindflipper stretched to show webbing and five nails. Steven Katona

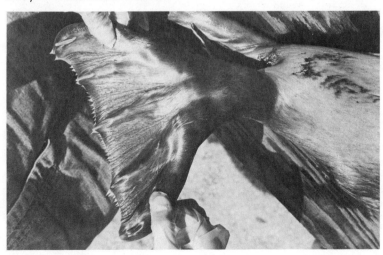

GRAY SEAL
(Halichoerus grypus)

Gray Seals on Ledge   D. D. Tyler
(females with light coats and males with dark coats), head of a swimming female
gray seal in background, Atlantic puffins in upper right

This is a large, imposing seal of remote, exposed islands,
reefs, and shoals. The distinctive Roman nose and gaping
nostrils become more pronounced with age, particularly in
males, whence the name "horsehead." The scientific name
(Gr. *halios*, marine, + *choiros*, pig, and Gr. *gropos*, hooknosed) means "hooknosed pig of the sea."

Males, or bulls, grow to 8 feet (244 cm) and 800 pounds
(362 kg) and the slightly smaller females, or cows, to 7 feet
(213 cm) and 400 pounds (181 kg). The donkeylike snout

is longer, broader, and more arched in males than in equal-aged females, although an old cow may have a convex profile. The massive appearance of a mature bull is enhanced by thick folds of leathery, scarred skin around the neck and shoulders. Males live to about 35 years and females to 45.

Immature gray seals may be confused with harbor seals of similar size; note, however, that the gray seal's eye is closer to the ear than to the nose, and the nostrils are well separated and, when viewed frontally, resemble a W rather than a V as in harbor seals.

Coat color pattern in gray seals is generally bolder and more coarsely spotted than in harbor seals. The male pelage usually has an overall dark tone of brown, gray, or nearly black, with small lighter-colored marks on the neck and flanks. The female coat has a light background, gray or tan on the back, and paler to silver or even white on the belly, with overlying dark spots and blotches. However, some females appear mostly dark. In younger seals of both sexes the pattern may be somewhat indistinct. The heads of most gray seals look brown when dry and dark gray when wet, but the common name does not refer to a unique quality, since other seals also look gray when wet.

Gray seals are found on both sides of the North Atlantic, with major populations in eastern Canada; northwestern Europe from Iceland to Norway, and around Great Britain; and the Baltic Sea. The western Atlantic stock centers in the Gulf of St. Lawrence, where ice breeding occurs in Northumberland Strait, George Bay, and near the Magdalen Islands. Outside the Gulf the seals breed on land, primarily in Nova Scotia at the Basque Islands and Sable Island, and also in small numbers on the east coast of Nova Scotia and near Grand Manan Island in the Bay of Fundy. The southernmost regular location of gray seals in North America is near Nantucket, Mass. Occasionally strays are seen south of New England.

The world population is about 135,000, over half of which live in the British Isles. Some 40,000 to 45,000 inhabit the Canadian Maritimes, and that stock is expanding. About 300 live in the Grand Manan archipelago, and probably

Gray Seal
D. D. Tyler

side view, male   front view, male   side view, female

fur pattern, male   fur pattern, female

Gray seal swimming at Flanders Bay, Maine, July 26, 1982. "Horsey" head contrasts with the doglike profile of harbor seals swimming nearby. Steven Katona

Gray seals at Sable Island, Nova Scotia. Left to right: pup, cow, bull. Geoff Beck

fewer than 300 along the Maine coast, with most sightings off Mt. Desert and Swans Islands and in lower Penobscot Bay. Gray seals select exposed haulout and breeding sites, usually where rough seas and riptides make boating hazardous; for this reason "horseheads" are seen infrequently except by fishermen. Occasionally individuals come ashore during the ice breeding season in the Gulf of St. Lawrence at places such as Prince Edward Island.

Gray seal bull, showing "horsehead." Sable Island, Nova Scotia. Geoff Beck

In eastern Canada pups are born in January and February on rocky or sandy islands or on land-fast ice. The newborn pup, averaging 3 feet (91 cm) and 36 pounds (16 kg), has a coat of long, creamy white hair (lanugo). It stays ashore for a nursing period of 2 to 3 weeks and may gain 4 to 5 pounds a day on its mother's high-fat milk, thus rapidly acquiring the vital layer of insulating blubber. In 2 to 3 weeks after birth the white coat is shed and a more or less variegated gray, brown, or black coat fairly similar to that of older seals develops. After weaning, pups may remain at the breeding ground for several more days or weeks until molting is complete.

The adults mate around the time of weaning. Sexually mature males (at least 3–5 years old) compete for females (mature at 3–4 years) to a variable degree. Where breeding occurs on rocky beaches, a few large vigorous bulls, probably over 8 years old, may be able to monopolize 4–6 cows apiece, but on sand or ice, cows are more spread out and each bull mates with only one. Competition among males probably contributes to their shorter life span.

Once molted, the pup enters the water if it has not done so previously, and learns to capture food on its own. Some pups may wander far from their birth places. First year mortality is about 50 percent. Molting in older seals takes place between March and June, followed by dispersal for summer feeding. Gray seals consume fish and invertebrates as available. The most common food items in eastern Canada are herring, cod, flounder, skate, squid, and mackerel.

If the Canadian stocks continue to grow, sightings in New England may become more common. It will be interesting to see whether such a trend develops.

HARP SEAL
(*Pagophilus groenlandicus*)

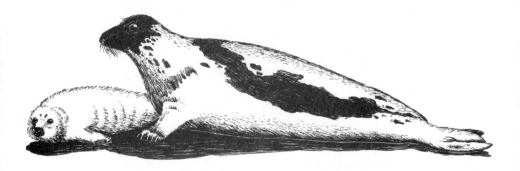

Harp Seals, adult and pup
approximate adult length: 6 feet
John R. Quinn

The beautiful harp seal, named for the dark harp- or saddle-shaped pattern on its back and flanks, is the most numerous seal in eastern Canada, yet it visits the Gulf of Maine only rarely.

Harp seals resemble harbor seals in body and head form, but are larger, to 6 feet (183 cm) and 400 pounds (182 kg) in both sexes, and proportionately stockier in the thoracic region. Fully mature males and females are whitish, silver, cream, or tan, with the head dark gray or black to just behind the eyes, and a series of dark blotches on the back forming the harp or saddle. These markings are most pronounced in males.

The pup from birth to 2½ weeks has a fine white fur, which it molts at 3 to 4 weeks for a gray coat with dark spots known in the fur trade as the "beater coat." Older immatures whose spots have grown larger are known as "bedlamers." In females the bedlamer stage lasts into early maturity and is followed by development of a pale saddle that progressively darkens in a few more years. In contrast, males acquire a dark saddle within 2 years of adulthood.

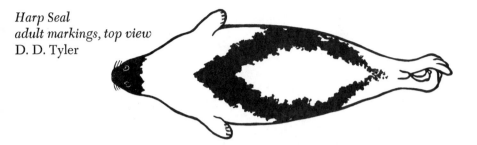

Harp Seal
adult markings, top view
D. D. Tyler

Females usually mature at age 4 or 5 years, but occasionally as early as 3 years or as late as 7 years. Males mature at the same age as females or a year or two later. Longevity is about 30 years.

Harp seals are found in the North Atlantic, in three main groups: (1) a western group in eastern Canada and western Greenland (territory of Denmark); (2) a central group associated with east Greenland, Spitzbergen, and Jan Mayen; and (3) an eastern group in the White Sea.

The northwest Atlantic harp seals have a complex annual cycle of migration and reproduction. They winter and breed on pack ice in the Gulf of St. Lawrence and off eastern Labrador. Then in late spring they follow the retreating ice northward, arriving at Baffin Island and southwest Greenland by early summer. Later in summer the seals reach Ellesmere Island and some also enter Hudson Bay to the west. Their close relationship to the ice is commemorated in the species name, from the Greek *pagos*, ice, and *philos*, loving— hence "the ice-loving seal of Greenland."

After a summer of feeding in the far north, adults and some immatures swim southward ahead of the advancing ice, feeding as they go. The seals reach Cape Chidley, the northern tip of Labrador, by mid-October, and the Strait of Belle Isle, separating Labrador from Newfoundland, in December. At the peak of the southward migration along the Atlantic coast of Labrador, shore viewers may see a continuous procession of swimming and porpoising seals, a sight that two hundred years ago was a vast spectacle, filling the sea to the horizon.

At the Strait of Belle Isle the migrating stream divides,

one-third of the seals entering the Gulf of St. Lawrence to feed, and the rest continuing south to feed near the Grand Bank. By mid-February well-nourished females seek out large areas of pack ice suitable for pupping, either in the Gulf of St. Lawrence near the Magdalen Islands or at the "Front" off Labrador and northeast Newfoundland, where the largest herds are found.

Pups averaging 40 inches (102 cm) long are born from late February to mid-March, those in the Gulf a few days earlier than those at the Front. The whitecoat pup about triples its birth weight of 26 pounds (12 kg) after 16 to 18 days of nursing. From 2½ to 4 weeks, as the white hair is falling out and the beater coat is growing in, the pup is known as a "ragged jacket." Weaning occurs at about 2½ weeks, and the female then mates, usually in the water, with one or more males in the vicinity.

At 4 weeks the newly molted pup, or beater, starts to swim and feed. In April and May older seals haul out in great herds on the Front ice to molt and fast for several weeks; Gulf seals, however, may molt in the water. Finally all the seals embark on the long northward migration of early summer. Only occasionally do individual harp seals stray south of the normal range to the Gulf of Maine and as far as Virginia.

Adult harp seals, which may dive to 137 fathoms, feed mainly on capelin and polar cod, and to a lesser degree on herring, cod, and planktonic crustaceans such as shrimp. The diet of immatures consists largely of krill and other shrimp-like crustaceans.

Populations of harp seals are difficult to estimate. There is little doubt that tens of millions lived in the North Atlantic before 1800, but overexploitation after that date drastically reduced the species stocks. Today the northwest Atlantic population (in eastern Canada and western Greenland) is thought to be between 1.8 and 2.4 million.

Estimates of pup production are the basis for management of the stocks. Each year quotas are set for the combined Canadian–Norwegian hunt at the Front, at which over 100,000 harp seals, primarily whitecoats and beaters, are

taken for furs and oil. Some are also processed as meat. In the Gulf of St. Lawrence, particularly at the Magdalen Islands, a smaller, less predictable number of harp seal pups are taken by "landsmen" operating on foot or in small boats.

Arctic Eskimos and Greenland natives harvest fewer than 12,000 animals of various ages during the harp seals' northern summer sojourn, and another 1,000 to 2,000 are taken in landsmen's nets during the December migration through the Strait of Belle Isle.

Harp seals on the Gulf of St. Lawrence ice pack during March pupping season. Two adult females are in the foreground, and a "whitecoat" pup is at the rear.
Fred Bruemmer

Projections of sustainable yield must be based on realistic population estimates, for only careful management will ensure this species' continued survival. The value of harp seals lies not only in pelts and meat but also in aesthetic appeal and the species' role in the ecosystem. There are now popular tours to the Magdalen Islands in late winter and early spring. Visitors see the islands, sample local culture, and, as weather permits, travel out onto the ice pack to view and photograph the seals.

HOODED SEAL
(Cystophora cristata)

Hooded Seals
approximate length: male, 10 feet; female, 9 feet
John R. Quinn

Hooded seals share much of the harp seals' range, but feed on larger prey in deeper water, and breed on older, heavier ice to seaward of harp seal herds at the Front off Labrador and northeastern Newfoundland. Compared with harp seals, hooded seals are uncommon, and their biology and ecology are not well understood.

The hooded seal is large and distinctive in appearance. Males grow to 9 feet (274 cm) and 900 pounds (408 kg); females are somewhat smaller, to 7 feet (213 cm) and 670 pounds (303 kg). Both sexes mature at 4 to 6 years, and longevity is about 20 years.

Coat pattern is identical in both sexes: the background is bluish gray, overlaid with irregular black patches several inches square, and with smaller spots on the belly. The face is black. The head is relatively larger and the muzzle heavier than the harbor seal's, with a broader, more flattened nostril area. The claws are substantial.

The species' most remarkable feature is the nasal apparatus of the male. Part of the nasal cavity is enlarged to form a distensible hood running from the crown to the upper lip, which it overhangs, proboscislike, in older animals. When the seal is angered, this structure can be inflated into a crest almost twice the size of a football. In addition, there is an inflatable nasal membrane that can be blown through the nostril as a red, balloonlike sac. The species' scientific and common names refer to these structures: the scientific name (Gr. *kostis*, bladder, + *phoros*, to carry, and L. *crista*, crest) translates as "bladder carrying seal with a crest." The function of this apparatus is not well documented or understood.

Small breeding units are found on drifting, heavy pack ice throughout the northernmost Atlantic, with three major concentrations. The largest is north of Iceland, at the so-called West Ice. Another group breeds on seaward pack ice at the Front off Labrador and northeastern Newfoundland, and in the Gulf of St. Lawrence. A third group, in Davis Strait near the Arctic Circle, was recently rediscovered.

Pups are born from mid-March to mid-April, and suckling lasts about 12 days. Mating occurs near the end of lac-

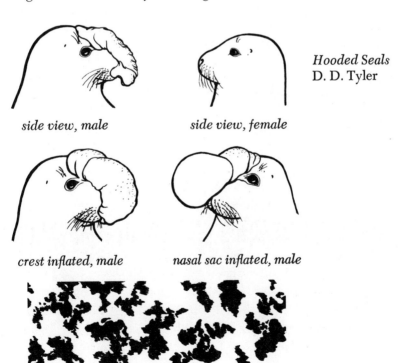

side view, male *side view, female*

Hooded Seals
D. D. Tyler

crest inflated, male *nasal sac inflated, male*

fur pattern

Hooded seal male, close-up of crest.
Geoff Beck

Hooded seal male, crest expanded.
Geoff Beck

tation. There may be from one to seven adult males on an ice floe with a female and pup. These "family units" are widely scattered and difficult to census. Numbers at the Front are variable, reaching the highest levels in years when cold and ice conditions are most severe.

The newborn pup, called a "blueback," is about 3.5 feet long (107 cm) and weighs about 51 pounds (23 kg). The exceptionally beautiful natal fur is slate blue on the back and light gray on the belly; the face is black. Under a yearly quota system blueback and adult hooded seals are hunted commercially, chiefly for pelts but also for meat and oil. In recent years the West Ice harvest has been set at 30,000 and the Canadian Front harvest at less than 20,000. The small Gulf of St. Lawrence herd and the Davis Strait group are completely protected. Small numbers of immatures are netted along the east coast of Labrador and the northeast coast of Newfoundland in winter. There is also a small unrestricted take of hooded seals by shore fishermen from Greenland in spring and summer.

After the breeding season the Canadian hooded seals migrate north, reaching west Greenland by late spring. Within a few weeks many turn and go southward again, later joining large molting assemblies east of Greenland in July and August.

Hooded seals tend to wander out of range, and stragglers often reach New England. A female and newborn pup were recorded at North Harpswell, Maine, in 1928; another such pair was seen at South Brooksville, Maine, in April 1974; and a third turned up at Wiscasset, Maine, in March 1982. In Canada, disoriented seals occasionally wander inland if pack ice fails during the breeding season. Individual hooded seals have been reported from Cape Cod to as far south as Florida.

Hooded seals eat redfish, Greenland turbot, octopus,

Hooded seal female and pup on the ice. Geoff Beck

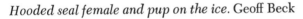

squid, herring, capelin, cod, shrimp, and mussels. Humans are the seals' greatest enemy, but ice accidents and predation by polar bears and possibly even killer whales and sharks also contribute to mortality.

The northwest Atlantic stock size is roughly estimated at about 150,000, but no recent comprehensive survey is available. As with harp seals, wise management is essential for the species' survival.

Hooded seal female in threat posture. This female and her newborn pup were seen at South Brooksville, Maine, April 10, 1974. R. Russell

RINGED SEAL
(*Phoca hispida*)

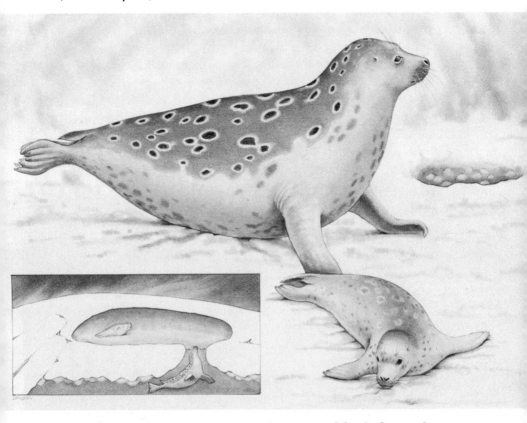

Ring seal mother and pup. Inset shows typical birth den in the ice.
Sarah Landry

This is the most common arctic seal and a mainstay of the
Eskimo economy. The ringed seal's distribution is circum-
polar, encompassing all of the Eurasian and Canadian arctic
and extending southward to Japan, Hudson Bay, Labrador,
and occasionally northeast Newfoundland and the Gulf of
St. Lawrence. There is also a group in the Baltic Sea.

Ringed seals are found wherever there is stable land-
fast ice in winter and spring, usually in fiords and bays but
also in some lakes and estuaries. Far offshore, drifting pack
ice may be occupied.

The ringed seal somewhat resembles a small harbor seal. Coat color is variable, generally consisting of a gray background with numerous dark spots, particularly on the back. Many of the spots are surrounded by light areas, forming the typical ringed pattern. The belly is silver. The ringed seal head looks similar to that of the harbor seal, but is shorter and narrower and tapers to a more pointed nose.

Size varies according to location and to stability of the ice conditions during the pupping season. Average adults range from 4 to 4.5 feet (122–137 cm) in length, and from 110 to 150 pounds (50–68 kg) in weight. Females are slightly smaller than males, though otherwise similar. Under optimum conditions an adult male may attain a maximum of 5 feet 5 inches (165 cm) and 250 pounds (113 kg).

During late fall and winter, mature seals live under the ice by maintaining breathing holes, while younger individuals stay at the open water edge of the ice. Pups are born from mid-March to mid-June in snow-covered lairs over breathing holes. The female excavates the birth lair out of a snowdrift or may use a space between rafted or uplifted ice blocks. The newborn pup has a long white lanugo coat, measures about 26 inches (66 cm), and weighs about 10 pounds (4.5 kg). Nursing may last for 6 to 8 weeks if the ice is sufficiently stable, but if early ice breakup terminates suckling, the stunted pup may not reach maximum size as an adult. Mating probably takes place from early March to late May and may occur within two weeks of the female's giving birth. There is evidence to suggest that the male, which has a strong, offensive odor during the breeding season, may overwinter with the female. An outmoded scientific name, *Pusa (Phoca) foetida*, referred to the male's odor.

The ringed seal pup starts to shed the white lanugo at about 3 weeks and develops a fine silvery coat. Such newly molted young are known as "silver jars," and yield prime pelts for the Eskimo fur trade. In June and July the older seals molt and fast, hauling out to bask near breathing holes or at the ice edge. The hair coats of older seals are coarse and worth less in the fur trade than those of the silver jars. The present species name, from the Latin *hispidus*,

Young adult ringed seal on the coast of northern Baffin Island, arctic Canada. Males and females are virtually identical. Fred Bruemmer

meaning rough and bristly, refers to the coarse hair texture. The breakup of the fast ice in July terminates the molting haulout, and summer feeding commences. Diet consists primarily of small shrimplike organisms and small polar cod.

Ringed seals, in their turn along the food chain, are killed by men, polar bears, killer whales, arctic foxes, and occasionally walruses. The birth lair provides the pup with vital shelter from such predation. With luck the ringed seal may live to 40 years, but a life span of 20 to 25 years is more usual. Females mature at 4 to 6 years and males at 5 to 7 years.

The worldwide population of ringed seals may number in the millions, with at least several hundred thousand in Canadian waters. However, the growing demand for furs could lead to overexploitation in certain localities, and a limited management program may become necessary in Canada.

ATLANTIC WALRUS
(*Odobenus rosmarus rosmarus*)

Walruses
approximate length: male, 10 feet; female, 8 feet
John R. Quinn

The walrus is a very rare visitor to eastern Canada south of Labrador today. This is a result of overexploitation by early European settlers and seafarers, for walruses were abundant farther south in early historic times. Until the eighteenth century several thousands inhabited the Gulf of St. Lawrence, notably the Magdalen Islands, and Nova Scotia as far south as Sable Island. Now there are probably fewer than 10,000 in all of eastern subarctic and arctic Canada, ranging from Hudson Strait, Hudson Bay, and Foxe Basin north to Ellesmere Island and as far west as Barrow Strait. This northwest Atlantic stock, comprising the Canadian group and about 6,000 walruses of north and west Greenland, is probably the last stronghold of the Atlantic walrus subspecies, the great stocks of the Eurasian arctic having been all but eliminated. On the other hand, the walrus is flourishing in the Alaskan and Siberian arctic, where between 200,000 and 250,000 remain.

The walrus is the largest North Atlantic pinniped and would not be mistaken easily for any other species. Characteristic features are great size; somewhat square-shaped head; small, often bloodshot eyes; large mustache pads bristling with hundreds of stout sensory whiskers; and, of course, long, ever-growing tusks. The skin is brownish-black with a sparse covering of reddish-brown hair.

Adult males may reach 10 feet (3 m) and 2,455 pounds (1,103 kg). The massiveness of the bull's neck and shoulders is accentuated by thick, lumpy skin. Females are smaller, reach a length of 8.5 feet (2.6 m) and a weight of 1,630 pounds (739 kg), and have a relatively smaller head with tusks more slender than the male's. There are four teats.

Tusks, elongated upper canine teeth, first form at 4 months of age and reach 1 inch (2.5 cm) at 1 year, 4 inches (10 cm) at 2 years, and 11 inches (28 cm) at 5 years. Adult tusks of up to 40 inches (100 cm) and 12 pounds (5.4 kg) have been recorded. The genus name (Gr. *odous*, tooth, + *baino*, I walk) suggests that the tusks help the walrus to walk. Since walruses may use their tusks to pull themselves up onto ice floes, the genus name is somewhat descriptive. Tusks are also used in threat displays and aggressive encounters between males, and, in both sexes, for defense against predators. The species name is from Norwegian *rossmaal* or *rossmar* and earlier Scandinavian words meaning "whale horse." One can imagine early Viking explorers attempting to describe this bizarre animal and meeting some success with "whale horse."

Another unique feature is a pair of pouches, part of the elastic pharynx, which extend back laterally between the neck muscles. If a walrus in the water is sleeping or wounded, the pouches may be inflated to act as buoys. In males, the pouches also produce a remarkable bell-like sound, heard most often during periods of sexual activity. One selection on the photograph record *Callings*, listed in the Bibliography, features that sound.

Calves, weighing 120 pounds (54 kg) and measuring almost 4 feet (122 cm), are born from April to June. The period of maternal care lasts about 2 years, and the mother's attentiveness and protectiveness are well known. The calf is often carried clinging to her back.

Females first breed at 4 to 7 years and bear young every 2 years at first, while older females tend to give birth at intervals of 3 years or longer. Males may mature at 6 years but usually do so at 9 or 10. Longevity ranges from 16 to 30 years.

The highly gregarious walrus favors a habitat of sea ice floating above shallow shellfish beds. The affinity for pack ice adjacent to temporary patches of open water persists year round in the most northern areas, but where ice breaks up in summer, walruses may haul out at traditional island sites that Eskimos call *uglit*. For most of the year, adult

Two adult male Atlantic walruses on Coats Island, in northern Hudson Bay. Male on right has a broken tusk. Fred Bruemmer

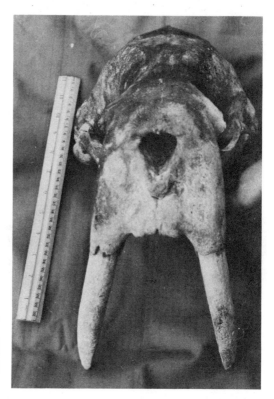

Skull of young walrus recovered from Chandler River, Machias, Maine, by Darrel Richards, June 1976. David Richardson

males herd separately from females and immatures. Mating occurs from January to March and apparently is promiscuous. Molting takes place from June until early fall.

Clams, the principal food, are obtained by digging in soft bottom with the tusks and bristles. The meat is sucked or torn from the shell before being swallowed. Other dietary items include whelks, sea cucumbers, worms, crustaceans, and small polar cod. Some individuals may eat belugas and narwhals, and possibly even ringed or bearded seals, either fresh or as carrion.

Walruses have few enemies except man. Although the young or infirm might fall prey to killer whales or polar bears, the exceptionally ferocious and aggressive adults are seldom molested.

Traditionally, Eskimos have hunted walrus for meat, oil, and hides, and this native hunt continues for subsistence purposes under a licensed quota system. Losses due to sinking add to hunting mortality, an important consideration because the species is slow to reproduce and its stocks are depleted. Oil and gas exploration in the Canadian arctic portend further threats to walruses as well as other organisms.

Sightings of walruses south of northern Labrador are of great interest. A live walrus was seen at Bear Cove, Nova Scotia, in the Bay of Fundy in 1937, and another appeared at Cape Sable, Nova Scotia, in 1976. Fossil bones, some dating back to the last ice age, have been found in New England and as far south as Georgia. Other bones recovered in New England may be those of individuals that strayed south of the normal range in more recent times.

Common Name Species	Length Nose to Tail Male, Female	Maximum Adult Weight	Coat, Fur	Head
Harbor seal (*Phoca vitulina*)	M 5–6 ft. 152– 183 cm F 4.5– 5.5 ft. 137– 168 cm	250 lb. 113 kg Same as male	Variable; light gray, tan, brown, or red, irregularly spotted with black. Pups born with gray or tan fur.	Short snout: forehead profile concave (doglike). Eye about equidistant from tip of nose and ear. Nostrils form a broad V almost meeting at bottom.
Gray seal (*Halichoerus grypus*)	M 8 ft. 244 cm F 7 ft. 213 cm	800 lb. 362 kg 400 lb. 181 kg	Variable; general rule is females light gray or brown background with dark patches; males dark brown gray or black with small, light markings. Pups born with embryonal white fur ("whitecoat").	Long snout with profile of forehead and snout straight or convex ("Roman nose"). Head donkey-shaped ("horsehead"). Eye closer to ear than nose. Nostril slits form a W when viewed from the front. Female has a smaller head than male.
Harp seal (*Pagophilus groenlandicus*)	M 6 ft. 183 cm F Same as male	400 lb. 182 kg Same as male	Pups born in "whitecoat"; juvenile coat spotted on gray or tan; mature adults may have distinct dark harp or horseshoe pattern on back and flanks.	Streamlined, doglike muzzle similar to harbor seal. Head and face dark in color compared with neck and chest.

Common Name Species	Length Nose to Tail Male, Female	Maximum Adult Weight	Coat, Fur	Head
Hooded seal (*Cystophora cristata*)	M 9 ft. 274 cm F 7 ft. 213 cm	900 lb. 408 kg 670 lb. 303 kg	"Blueback" pups have silver-bluish-gray back with white belly; adults gray with distinct black patches of irregular shape; black muzzle and face.	Larger and heavier muzzle than harbor seal, with broader, more flattened nostril area when viewed from front. Crest of hood on top of head and muzzle of mature male. Inflatable nasal sac in male.
Ringed seal (*Phoca hispida*)	M 4–5.5 ft. 122–168 cm F slightly smaller	150–250 lb. 68–113 kg slightly smaller	Variable; generally a gray background with numerous dark spots surrounded by light areas, forming ringed pattern. Pups born in "whitecoat."	Similar to harbor seal head but smaller, with more pointed snout.
Walrus (*Odobenus rosmarus rosmarus*)	M 10 ft. 304 cm F 8 ft. 244 cm	2,000 lbs. 907 kg 1,250 lbs. 567 kg	Rough, wrinkled skin with very sparse reddish brown hair.	Short, squarish head with large white tusks and stiff whiskers (both sexes). Pharyngeal pouches in neck area.

SAMPLE SEAL CENSUS AND SIGHTING REPORT FORM

Please report all seals seen on (or about) any or all of these dates: February 1, March 15, April 15, May 25, August 15, December 15; also report the absence of seals usually seen along your course or at traditional sites. In case of poor weather, take your census on the next clear day. Gray and harbor seals should be censused at low tide.

In addition to censuses on these dates, we welcome your observations at other times of the year and encourage you, when possible, to identify individual seals by natural markings (pigmentation and scars) and/or by tags and brands.

Please use a separate sheet, on which sightings may be listed consecutively, for each species. A suggested format for data collection is shown below.

Your name _____   Address _____   Seal species _____

SIGHTINGS

| Date | Time | Location | Number of Seals | | State of Tide | Weather* | Comments** |
			Hauled Out	In Water			
___	___	___	___	___	___	___	___
___	___	___	___	___	___	___	___

* Air temperature, visibility, sun, wind speed and direction, sea condition, and sea surface temperature.
** Group composition (size, sex); behavior; special markings, tags or brands; etc.
Send to: Allied Whale, College of the Atlantic, Bar Harbor, Maine 04609.

PLEASE REPORT ALL TAGS AND BRANDS SEEN, AND
ANY WALRUSES SOUTH OF NORTHERN LABRADOR,
TO:

IF SEEN IN CANADA

Brian Beck, Marine Fish Division
Bedford Institute of Oceanography
P.O. Box 1006
Dartmouth, Nova Scotia
B2Y 4A2 CANADA

IF SEEN IN UNITED STATES

Allied Whale
College of the Atlantic
Bar Harbor, Maine 04609
U.S.A.

APPENDICES

Important Prey Species of Whales, Porpoises, and Seals

A LIST OF EVERY ANIMAL THAT SOMETIMES OCCURS IN THE DIET of whales, porpoises, or seals within our study area would probably include many dozens of species. Nearly all of these animals will feed on whatever prey is abundant and can be taken with the anatomical and behavioral feeding adaptations they possess. So it is no surprise that they tend to use as principal prey species those fishes or invertebrates that are most abundant in our study area. Staple foods for various marine mammals in our study area include the copepod *Calanus finmarchicus;* the krill (*Meganyctiphanes norvegica* and *Thysanoessa* spp.); capelin (*Mallotus villosus*); herring (*Clupea harengus*); sand launce (*Ammodytes americanus*); mackerel (*Scomber scombrus*); and the short-finned squid (*Illex illecebrosus*). Brief life histories of these important species may help the reader to understand the feeding ecology of the whales and seals that eat them.

Calanus finmarchicus is found throughout the temperate waters of the Northern Hemisphere. It is the most abundant herbivorous planktonic copepod in the North Atlantic Ocean and is the chief food for many common fish species at some stage in their development. An adult *Calanus* is about 0.2 inch (5 mm) long, and about 200,000 of them would weigh 1 pound (454 gm). During a day each adult could filter the tiny planktonic plant cells from about half a cup of water. The life cycle includes twelve developmental stages, and several generations may be produced each year under favorable circumstances. During early spring, immature males and females that have spent the winter in the eleventh developmental stage (Stage V copepodite) at depths of about 50 fathoms or more become active again and migrate to the surface to feed on the new growth of planktonic plant cells. They mature and mate, and the females lay fertilized eggs in the surface layers. The eggs hatch, and the resulting teardrop-shaped nauplius larva molts six times, eventually becoming a miniature adult that grows during six more molts to full size. Total development time from egg to ripe female adult is about 2½ months during spring and summer in the Gulf of Maine. This species is the main food of right whales and basking sharks and is also important in the diet of sei whales. Even finback whales and minke whales may take *Calanus* on occasion. Certain sea birds, notably Wilson's petrel, Leach's petrel, and the northern and red phalaropes, feed on *Calanus*, and the sight of these birds busily dipping their bills into the water is a good clue that copepods are present near the surface.

Calanus is frequently abundant enough to completely dominate a plankton net haul taken in coastal waters, filling the sample bottle with a nearly solid mass of copepods. We have spread them on bread, and they taste like a shrimp pâté. Attempts have been made to harvest *Calanus* for human consumption by anchoring large plankton nets in Norwegian fjords to strain the copepods from the tidally flowing waters, but yields were not sufficient for commercial operations.

The life cycles of two of the krill species important in our study area, *Meganyctiphanes norvegica* and *Thysanoessa inermis*, are quite similar. Mating occurs in late spring, with a peak in June. Eggs are released in early July, and larvae molt and grow through September. Little growth occurs in winter, but further growth and sexual maturation take place in spring as planktonic plants (phytoplankton) become abundant. Both sexes can survive to mate a second time the following summer. Both species attain maximum adult lengths of about 1½ inches (38 mm) and fresh weights of perhaps 600 to a pound (750 mg each).

Immature stages, especially, of both species swarm at the surface during summer in some locations where upwelling occurs, but these swarms do not achieve the extraordinary abundance of Antarctic species. In fact, little is known about the absolute abundance of krill in our study area, because they are very difficult to catch in nets. Their compound eyes can easily see an approaching net, especially if any luminescent organisms (including the krill themselves) have been caught, for then the net shows up better; the krill are able to swim fast enough to get out of the way. Furthermore, adults usually spend daylight hours on or very close to the bottom, which presents additional sampling problems for towed nets. We do not know how the baleen whales, all of which feed on krill to some extent, manage to catch them so much more efficiently than we can. Other creatures whose diet depends heavily on krill at times include, among others, cod, herring and capelin, mackerel, seals, and sea birds. We have dipped krill from surface swarms in Passamaquoddy Bay, eaten them raw, and found them to have a delicious crablike flavor.

Herring is one of the most important bait fishes in the southern half of our study area, especially in the Gulf of Maine, along the Nova Scotia coast, and in the Gulf of St. Lawrence. Herring feed predominantly on zooplankton, especially *Calanus* and other copepods, plus the krill species. The western North Atlantic population is apparently broken up into many local spawning stocks, whose location and size may be determined largely by the existence of current patterns that retain the larvae in the spawning areas. Major spawning areas include Georges Bank, the southeast coast of Nova Scotia,

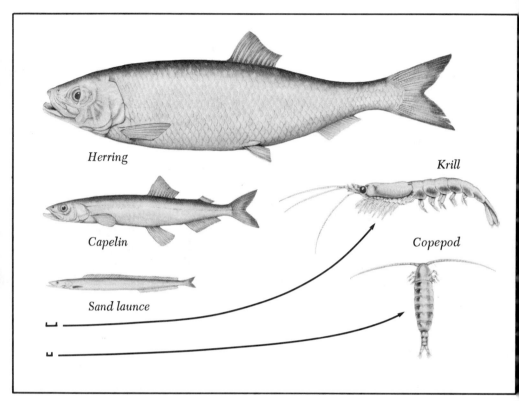

Important Prey Species

shoals southwest of Grand Manan Island, and several locations on the south shore of the Gulf of St. Lawrence. Adult herring, usually over 4 years old and 10 inches (25 cm) long, spawn during late August and September in the Gulf of Maine. A female may lay about 30,000 eggs on average. The sticky eggs sink and remain in place on the bottom close to the coast. The eggs hatch in about 2 weeks into larvae the size of a large *Calanus*. By Christmas they are 1 or 2 inches (25–50 mm) long; by June, 2 to 2½ inches (50–63 mm) long. At age 1 year the 3- to 5-inch (76–127 mm) fish are called brit, and at this size they first become choice food for whales, porpoises, seals, and sea birds. During summer and autumn, schools of brit and older herring feed in coastal waters, often close to shore, rising to the surface about dawn and dusk to catch plankton. The fish continue to grow to 9 or 10 inches (23–25 cm) by age 3 years and about 1 foot (30 cm) at age 7. Herring can live to be 20 years old, 17

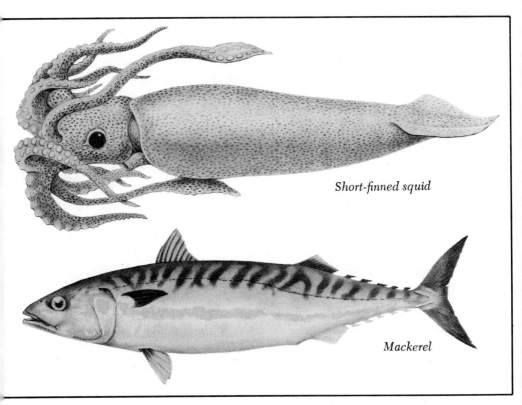

Short-finned squid

Mackerel

Sarah Landry

inches (43 cm) long, and about 1.5 pounds (680 gm) in weight, though most will be eaten much earlier. Although herring populations rise and fall with the variable success of spawning, an indication of the extraordinary potential abundance is given by the total catch for the Gulf of Maine in 1928, when over a quarter of a billion pounds, representing probably 5 or 6 billion fish, were harvested.

The capelin is the chief baitfish of arctic and subarctic portions of the North Atlantic Ocean. It is smaller and slimmer than a herring, growing to only 6.5 or 7.5 inches (16–19 cm) and running perhaps six to the pound (75 gm each). Capelin spend most of the year at sea, but form vast schools that come inshore to spawn, usually at night, when water temperature is from 40° to 47°F. (4.4°–8.3°C). Spawning starts in June along the Newfoundland coast and in July or August in Labrador. Fish spawn from just below the wave line of beaches out to depths of up to 25 fathoms. Females lay up to 50,000 small (.04-inch, or 1-mm) red eggs that stick to the bottom and hatch in about 2 weeks. After spawning, the spent adults form large but listless schools that fall easy prey to humpback, finback, and minke whales, as well as seals, sea birds, and fishes such as cod. Some capelin survive to mate a second or third time. A capelin will be about 3.5 inches (9 cm) long at 1 year of age and will begin to spawn at age 3 or 4. Throughout its life it will feed mainly on copepods, especially *Calanus,* and krill. During the late 1960s and early 1970s, European fleets began to harvest the offshore population of capelin on the Grand Bank for use as human food, dog food, fertilizer, and fishmeal. After several years of heavy fishing, the Grand Bank capelin catch fell sharply, perhaps because of overfishing. At about the same time, humpback whales began to appear inshore in increasing numbers during summer along the Newfoundland coast, feeding on inshore populations of capelin, which were still abundant. The whales caused a great deal of damage to coastal fishing gear, and in the process up to at least several dozen humpbacks per year drowned or were shot after becoming entangled in nets. Temporary closure of the Grand Bank capelin fishery and fishing gear modifications will, it is hoped, lead to a reduction in humpback entanglements.

The sand launce (also called sand eel) is extraordinarily important in the diet of whales, porpoises, sea birds, and commercial fishes such as cod, haddock, mackerel, hake, and others. On shoal banks with sandy bottoms, these little fish (maximum 7 inches, or 18 cm) occur in dense schools during spring through autumn, feeding mainly on copepods. They can be recognized in the water by their eellike undulations while swimming. Sand launce frequently bury themselves 4 to 6 inches (10–15 cm) deep in the sand, perhaps to avoid predators or, in very shallow locations, to avoid dessication when the tide is out. Sand launce are found in abundance in the southern part of the Gulf of Maine, on Georges and Browns banks, in the Gulf of St. Lawrence, and along the Newfoundland and Labrador coasts. During the winter some fish may migrate into somewhat deeper water. Spawning appears to take place during autumn and early winter, with eggs sticking to sand grains at depths of about 10 fathoms. The young launce grow to about 3 or 4 inches (7–10 cm) in their first year and may mature during the second year. Adults average 4 to 6 inches (10–15 cm) in length, and 6-inch fish might run about twenty-five to the pound (18 gm each). There is no fishery for sand launce at present, although some consideration has been given to developing one in the southern Gulf of Maine.

Mackerel, *Scomber scombrus*, roam the coastal waters of the southern part of our study area during the warmer months, but their abundance and distribution are more variable than in the other bait fishes. In some summers enormous numbers of mackerel are present, with schools of many thousands rippling the surface in all directions. In other years few mackerel can be found. Large schools nearly always appear in the Gulf of Maine from Georges Bank to Cape Cod and Jeffreys Ledge, but abundance declines farther east. The fish again become abundant along the outer Nova Scotia coast and in the southern Gulf of St. Lawrence, tapering off in Newfoundland waters. Wherever they are abundant, mackerel eat most suitably sized planktonic animals, especially crustaceans, or small fishes, notably herring and sand launce. In turn they become the food for fish such as sharks, tuna, and bluefish; seals; porpoises and some whales; and sea birds such as gannets. During winter the mackerel schools apparently migrate to deeper water over the continental shelf offshore from Virginia to Nova Scotia. Reappearance along the coasts occurs rather unpredictably during spring or summer, sometime after the water warms to over 46°F (7.8°C). After the mackerel have fed voraciously for several months, spawning takes place at temperatures from 48°F to 57°F (9–14°C). A typical female weighing 1.5 pounds (680 gm) may release up to one-half million eggs in batches of 50,000 or so over a period of some weeks. Eggs are broadcast and fertilized externally wherever the fish happen to be. Many of the mackerel that summer in our study area have already spawned south of Cape Cod. The free-floating eggs hatch in about six days at 55°F (13°C). The larvae, only

0.125 inch (3 mm) long, usually grow to 8 or 9 inches (20–23 cm) in length by autumn, when they migrate offshore. By the next autumn they are 12 to 13 inches (30–33 cm) long, and 14 to 15 inches (36–38 cm) in their third autumn. Most mackerel spawn the following summer at age 3 years, and every summer thereafter until they die. Potential longevity is at least 8 or 10 years.

The short-finned squid, *Illex illecebrosus*, is important in the food web of our study area, both as a predator on herring, capelin, and mackerel and as food for pilot whales, other odontocetes, seals, and sea birds, especially fulmars and shearwaters. As is usually the case with squid, this species grows very quickly, breeding and then dying at the end of one year. Within that single year, a typical male will have grown to a mantle length, tentacles excluded, of 1 foot (30 cm) and a weight of 12 ounces (340 gm), and a female will have reached 14 inches (36 cm) and 18 ounces (510 gm). A herring would take 4 years to reach the same size. From Newfoundland and southern Labrador to Massachusetts, this squid comes inshore during late spring to feed on schooling fish. From May to November the weight of a typical individual will increase eightfold or tenfold in the productive coastal waters. During late autumn, the mature squid apparently swim offshore to spawn in deep water at the edge of the continental shelf, and most of them probably die shortly thereafter. Small squid feed on zooplankton, especially krill, while in offshore waters, then gradually switch to a fish diet as they grow and come inshore. Hundreds of tons of short-finned squid are caught along the Newfoundland and Nova Scotia coasts for use as bait in the long-line fishery for cod and other ground fish. The squid are caught with jigs, either by hand or with large mechanized reels. The related squid species *Loligo pealii* is caught for human food in the southern part of the Gulf of Maine and south of Cape Cod, largely for the Chinese, Portuguese, and Italian markets. *Illex illecebrosus* is every bit as good, and is not eaten only because squid is not part of the traditional diet of northern New England or eastern Canada.

PART 1

Whale-Watching Excursions

Massachusetts

Capt. Al Avellar
The Dolphin Fleet
Macmillan Wharf
Provincetown, MA 02657
(617) 487-1900 (summer)
(617) 255-3857 (off
  season)

Four-hour trips, three times daily, spring through autumn, to Stellwagen Bank, with naturalists supplied by the Provincetown Center for Coastal Studies.

Barnegat Transportation
Pickering Wharf
Salem, MA 01970
(617) 745-6070

Half-day trips on weekends in May and September, and Tuesday through Sunday from Memorial Day to Labor Day, aboard M/V *New England Star.*

M/V *Cape Cod Princess*
Mayflower II
State Pier
Municipal Pier
Plymouth, MA 02360
(617) 747-2400

Half-day and full-day cruises from May 1 through October 12, with onboard slide presentation by naturalist. This company, Princess Cruise Lines, also offers four-day trips from June through September, leaving from Fisherman's Wharf Marina, Provincetown; (617) 487-2274.

M/V *Capt. John and Son*
Town Wharf
Plymouth, MA 02360
(617) 746-2643

Day trips, spring through summer, to Stellwagen Bank.

Gloucester Fisherman's
  Museum
Cetacean Research Unit
Rogers and Porter Sts.
Box 159
Gloucester, MA 01930
(617) 283-1940

Daily morning and afternoon trips on several boats, spring through autumn.

Gloucester Sightseeing
  Cruises, Inc. and Cape
  Ann Whale Watch
12 Clarendon St.
Gloucester, MA 01930
(617) 283-5110

Half-day trips, twice daily, May through autumn, accompanied by naturalists from the Gloucester Fisherman's Museum.

Gloucester Whalewatch
(The Yankee Fleet)
75 Essex Ave., Rte. 133
Gloucester, MA 01930
(617) 283-6089

Half-day trips, twice daily, spring through autumn.

Greenpeace New
  England
286 Congress St.
Boston, MA 02210
(617) 542-8107

Organizes day trips from Provincetown and north and south shores of Massachusetts.

New England Aquarium
Central Wharf
Boston, MA 02110
(617) 742-8830

Day trips, spring, summer, and early autumn.

Pelagic Systems Research
J. Michael Williamson,
  Dir.
Box 213
Beverly Farms, MA 01915
(617) 468-7147

Organizes six- and eight-hour trips from Boston and Salem, spring through autumn.

M/V *Ranger III* and *IV*
Macmillan Pier
Provincetown, MA 02657
(617) 487-1582

Each boat runs two half-day trips, spring through autumn, to Stellwagen Bank.

Web of Life Outdoor
  Education Center
P.O. Box 530
Main St.
Carver, MA 02330
(617) 866-5353

Organizes half-day trips aboard M/V *Captain John and Son* from Plymouth, Mass., spring through autumn, with naturalist and slide orientation provided.

New Hampshire

Gauron Deep Sea Fishing
1 Ocean Blvd.
Hampton Beach, NH
  03842
(603) 926-2469

Two full-day trips each week from Hampton Beach to Jeffreys Ledge on Stellwagen Bank.

New Hampshire
  Whalewatch
Box 825
Hampton, NH 03842
(603) 926-0952

Day trips from New Hampshire ports and from Newburyport, Mass., April through October, accompanied by naturalist Scott Mercer.

Viking of Yarmouth
  Cruises
Viking Dock
Market St.
Portsmouth, NH 03801
(603) 431-5500

Weekend watching from early May through June 12 and from Sept. 10 through Oct. 10. Trips go to Jeffreys Ledge or Cape Ann.

Maine

Allied Whale
c/o College of the Atlantic
Bar Harbor, ME 04609
(207) 288-5015

Organizes day trips on several weekends, spring and autumn, from ports in Maine, New Hampshire, or Massachusetts.

Butch Huntley
M/V *Seafarer*
9 High St.
Lubec, ME 04652
(207) 733-5584

Full-day trips and charters from Lubec to Passamaquoddy Bay and lower Bay of Fundy, July through October.

Bob Bowman
Maine Whale Watch
Box 78
Northeast Harbor, ME
  04662
(207) 244-7429

Full-day cruises from Northeast Harbor, Mt. Desert Island, to observe whales, seals, and sea birds. Naturalist-led cruises aboard M/V *Island Queen* daily from June through September. Reservations may also be made through Beal and Bunker, Inc., Cranberry Isles, ME 04625; (207) 244-3575.

Seafarers
Box 428
RFD 1
Machias, ME 04654
(207) 255-8810

Week-long programs featuring naturalist-led day trips to observe whales and sea birds in the lower Bay of Fundy region.

Canada

Gerald Iles Enterprises
2053 Vendome Ave.
Montreal, Quebec
Canada, H4A 3M4

Day trips to Saguenay River region of Gulf of St. Lawrence.

Russ Kinne, Inc.
No. Wilton Rd.
New Canaan, CT 06840
(203) 966-4900 or
(212) 758-3420

Week-long trips in Gulf of St. Lawrence by boat and air.

Linnean Society of
  Quebec
Quebec Aquarium
1675 Ave. du Parc
Sainte-Foy, Quebec
Canada, G1W 4S3
(418) 653-8186

Day trips in Gulf of St. Lawrence and Saguenay River estuary, summer and autumn.

Mingan Islands
  Cetacean Study
C.P. 159
Sept Iles, Quebec
Canada G4R4K3 or
  P.O. Box 518
  Meriden, CT 06450

Ten-day programs of day trips around Mingan Islands, Gulf of St. Lawrence, to observe whales and sea birds.

Montreal Zoological
  Society
Montreal, Quebec
Canada H3A IV4
(514) 845-8317

Weekend trips to Saguenay River region of Gulf of St. Lawrence, August and September.

Ocean Contact, Ltd.
The Village Inn
P.O. Box 10
Trinity, Newfoundland
Canada, ADC 250
(709) 464-3269

Week-long programs with daily trips into Trinity Bay.

Ocean Search
Marathon Inn
North Head
Grand Manan Island
New Brunswick
Canada
(506) 662-8144

Trips in the lower Bay of Fundy, with one-, three-, four-, and seven-day packages during summer and early summer.

Extended Voyages

Dirigo Cruises
39 Waterside Lane
Clinton, CT 06413
(203) 669-7068

Week-long whale study cruises aboard schooner *Harvey Gamage* scheduled for summer 1983.

Earthwatch
Center for Field Research
10 Juniper Rd.
Box 127
Belmont, MA 02178
(617) 489-3030

Places volunteers on field research projects throughout the world. Opportunities to help in whale research projects vary annually.

Ocean Research and Education Society, Inc. (ORES)
19-29 Harbor Loop
Gloucester, MA 01930
(617) 523-3455

Research cruises throughout year studying whales in the Caribbean region, and in the Gulf of Maine, Newfoundland, and Greenland aboard 144-ft. barkentine R/V *Regina Maris.*

Sea Education Assoc., Inc.
P.O. Box 6
Woods Hole, MA 02543
(617) 540-3954

Undergraduate program in oceanography aboard 125-ft. R/V *Westward* with research cruises throughout the western North Atlantic Ocean. Some whale research on Silver and Navidad Banks, in the Gulf of Maine, Gulf of St. Lawrence, and en route.

School for Field Studies
50 Western Ave.
Cambridge, MA 02138
(617) 497-9000

Month-long creditworthy courses in various scientific disciplines, including marine mammal biology and cetacean behavioral ecology for undergraduates and advanced secondary students.

Wings, Inc.
Box 974
Northeast Harbor, ME 04662
(207) 276-5077

One three-day trip offshore to continental shelf break community to observe whales and seabirds during autumn.

Ferry Boats

Canadian National Marine
Eden St.
Bar Harbor, ME 04609
(800) 432-7344 (Maine)
(800) 341-7981 (eastern U.S.)
or
Canadian National Marine

A map of all ferry routes operated by CN Marine is on page 231. The names of vessels operating may change. Write or call the reservations bureau or the CN Marine office at any of the ports of call shown on the map for schedule information. Reservations for any vessel can be made from any CN office,

Canadian National Marine Ferry Routes

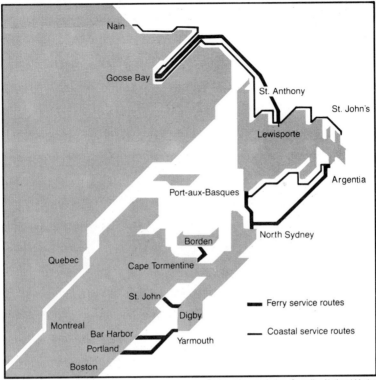

Nain
Goose Bay
St. Anthony
St. John's
Lewisporte
Argentia
Port-aux-Basques
North Sydney
Borden
Quebec
Cape Tormentine
St. John
Digby
Montreal
Bar Harbor
Portland
Yarmouth
Boston

■■■ Ferry service routes
――― Coastal service routes

Redrawn by permission, Canadian National Marine

P.O. Box 250
North Sydney, Nova
  Scotia
Canada B2A 3M3

which can usually be reached toll-free. Listings can be obtained by dialing (800) 555-1212.

M/V *Grand Manan*
Black's Harbor
New Brunswick, Canada

Service between Black's Harbor and North Head, Grand Manan Island. About 1½ hours each way.

M/V *Scotia Prince*
Prince of Fundy Cruises
International Terminal
Portland, ME 04101
(207) 775-5616 (Portland)
(902) 742-5164
  (Yarmouth)

Service between Portland and Yarmouth, Nova Scotia. Trip lasts about 10½ hours, with up to 8 hours of daylight on the Yarmouth-Portland leg.

Seal-Watching Excursions

New Hampshire

Viking of Yarmouth
Viking Dock
Market St.
Portsmouth, NH 03801
(603) 431-5500

Harbor seals can be observed at Duck Island, Isles of Shoals, during some whale-watching trips in spring, if tides are right.

Maine

Acadia Boat Tours and
   Charters, Inc.
Golden Anchor Pier
Bar Harbor, ME 04609
(207) 288-4324 (summer)
(207) 244-3625 (off
   season)

Short cruises to view seals on ledges in Frenchman Harbor, leaving from Golden Anchor Pier, Bar Harbor, daily from June through October.

Beal and Bunker, Inc. Cranberry Isles, ME 04625 (207) 244-3575	Three-hour cruises from Northeast Harbor, Mt. Desert Island, late June to September, emphasizing history and geography, but usually providing the opportunity to view harbor seals and sea birds.
Capt. John Earl M/V *Henrietta* Spruce Head, ME 04859 (207) 594-5411	Harbor seals are frequently seen during daily fishing trips to Matinicus islands group, mid-May to October 1.
Frenchman's Bay Boating Co. Bar Harbor, ME 04609 (207) 288-5741	Several times daily, Memorial Day through September, features harbor seals, porpoises, eagles, and ospreys.
Isleford Ferry Co. Isleford, ME 04646 (207) 244-3366 (summer) (603) 926-6005 (off season)	Nature and Baker's Island cruises, mid-June to mid-September, concentrate on natural and human history of area. Harbor seals and an osprey nest are often seen.
Maine Whale Watch Capt. Bob Bowman Box 78 Northeast Harbor, ME 04662 (207) 244-7429	Full-day cruises from Northeast Harbor, Mt. Desert Island, to observe whales, harbor seals, gray seals, and sea birds. Naturalist-led cruises aboard M/V *Island Queen* daily from June through September. Reservations may also be made through Beal and Bunker, Inc., Cranberry Isles, ME 04625; (207) 244-3575.
Mt. Katahdin Cruises Penobscot Bay Line P.O. 1112 Rockland, ME 04841 (207) 594-8416	Harbor seals may be seen on some cruises from spring through autumn.

Barna Norton
M/V *Chief*
Jonesport, ME 04649
(207) 497-5933

Charter trips from Jonesport to Machias Seal Island to view sea birds, harbor seals, and gray seals.

Vagabond Cruises
Bass Harbor, ME 04653
(207) 244-5365

Bass Harbor Naturalist Cruise emphasizes natural history. Sightings of harbor seals and gray seals are possible from June through September.

Canada

Hanns Ebensten Travel, Inc.
705 Washington St.
New York, NY 10014
(212) 691-7429

A March trip to view harp seals on the ice pack is scheduled annually, pending sufficient demand and favorable ice conditions in the Gulf of St. Lawrence.

Preston Wilcox
Seal Cove
Grand Manan Island
New Brunswick, Canada
(506) 662-8296

Gray seals and harbor seals and sea birds may be viewed during charter trips to Machias Seal Island.

Bibliography

SPECIES GUIDE TO THE BIBLIOGRAPHY ON CETACEANS, "BONUS" SPECIES, AND PREY SPECIES

General: 5, 7, 9, 13, 17, 21, 23, 24, 25, 26, 27, 29, 31, 35, 46, 47, 67, 68, 76, 79, 83, 84, 93, 96, 101, 111, 118

Mysticetes: 1, 6, 14, 17, 40, 54, 55, 65, 67, 69, 70, 71, 72, 73, 83, 85, 86, 87, 91, 102, 103, 110, 111, 118
Odontocetes: 15, 17, 40, 49, 50, 53, 54, 56, 57, 67, 68, 73, 76, 85, 86, 87, 92, 102, 106, 111, 118

Finback whale: 69, 70, 91, 94, 109, 110
Minke whale: 10, 45, 61, 70, 90, 116
Humpback whale: 30, 33, 34, 42, 43, 48, 69, 70, 71, 105, 110, 112, 113, 114, 115, 117
Right whale: 36, 58, 77, 82, 104, 110
Blue whale: 1, 86
Sei whale: 58, 62, 110

Harbor porpoise: 18, 19, 74, 75, 97, 99
Pilot whale: 51, 88, 89
White-sided dolphin: 20, 32, 81
White-beaked dolphin: 15, 40, 111
Common dolphin: 15, 40, 111
Striped dolphin: 63, 66
Bottlenose dolphin: 15, 40, 111
Gray grampus: 15, 40, 111
Killer whale: 2, 12
Beluga: 22, 78, 95
Sperm whale: 11, 44, 107, 108
Pygmy sperm whale: 14, 40
Northern bottlenose whale: 59, 60
Dense-beaked whale: 14, 111
True's beaked whale: 14, 111
North Sea beaked whale: 14, 40, 111

Basking shark: 3, 41
Ocean sunfish: 3, 41
Leatherback turtle: 4, 8, 16, 38, 39, 64, 73, 80
Prey species: 3, 28, 37, 41, 52, 100, 101, 119

I. CETACEANS, "BONUS" SPECIES, AND PREY SPECIES

1. Allen, G. M. 1916. "The Whalebone Whales of New England." *Mem. Boston Soc. Nat. Hist.* 8(2):1–322.
2. Balcomb, K. C., III; J. R. Boran; R. W. Osborne; N. J. Haenel; and S. L. Heimlich. 1980. "Killer Whales in Greater Puget Sound." In *A Mini-guide to Whales and Porpoises of the Inland Waters of Washington State.* Whale Museum, Friday Harbor, WA 98250. 30 pp.
3. Bigelow, H. B., and W. C. Schroeder, 1953. "Fishes of the Gulf of Maine." *Fish. Bull. Fish and Wildlife Service*, Vol. 53. Cambridge, Mass.: Museum of Comparative Zoology, Harvard Univ.
4. Bleakney, J. S. 1965. "Reports of Marine Turtles from New England and Canadian Waters." *Canadian Field. Nat.* 79(2):120–28.

5. Bonner, W. N. 1980. *Whales.* Poole, Dorset, England: Blandford Press. Distrib. in U.S. by Sterling Pub., N.Y.

6. Brodie, P. F. 1975. "Cetacean Energetics, an Overview of Intraspecific Size Variation." *Ecology* 50:152–61.

7. Brower, K. 1980. *Wake of the Whale.* N.Y.: Friends of the Earth.

8. Carr, A. 1984. *So Excellent a Fishe.* N.Y.: Scribners.

9. CETAP. 1981. *A Characterization of Marine Mammals and Turtles in the Mid- and North-Atlantic Areas of the U.S. Outer Continental Shelf.* Annual Report for 1979. Cetacean and Turtle Assessment Program, Univ. Rhode Island, Kingston, RI 02881, prepared for U.S. Dept. Interior, Bureau of Land Management, 18th and C Sts., N.W., Rm. 2455, Wash., D.C. 20240.

10. Christensen, I. 1981. "Age Determination of Minke Whales, *Balaenoptera acutorostrata*, from Laminated Structures in the Tympanic Bullae." *Rep. Int. Whal. Comm.* 31:245–53.

11. Clarke, M. R. 1979. "The Head of the Sperm Whale." *Sci. Amer.* 240(1):128–41.

12. Dahlheim, M. E. 1981. "A Review of the Biology and Exploitation of the Killer Whale, *Orcinus orca*, with Comments on Recent Sightings from Antarctica." *Rep. Int. Whal. Comm.* 31:541–46.

13. Dietz, T. 1982. *Tales of Whales.* Portland, Maine: Guy Gannet Pub. Co.

14. Ellis, R. 1980. *The Book of Whales.* N.Y.: Alfred A. Knopf.

15. ———. 1982. *Dolphins and Porpoises.* N.Y.: Alfred A. Knopf.

16. Frair, W.; R. E. Ackman; and N. Mrosovsky. 1972. "Body Temperature of *Dermochelys coriacea*: Warm Turtle from Cold Water." *Science* 177:791–93.

17. Gaskin, D. E. 1982. *The Ecology of Whales and Dolphins.* Exeter, N.H.: Heinemann Educational Books.

18. ———. 1977. "Harbor Porpoise (*Phocoena* [L.]) in the Western Approaches to the Bay of Fundy. 1969–75." *Rep. Int. Whal. Comm.* 27:487–92.

19. ———; P.W. Arnold; and B. A. Blair. 1974. "*Phocoena phocoena.*" *Mamm. Species* 42:1–8.

20. Geraci, J. R.; S. A. Testaverde; D. J. St. Aubin; and T. H. Loop. 1976. "A Mass Stranding of the Atlantic White-Sided Dolphin, *Lagenorhynchus acutus*: A Study into Pathobiology and Life History." Final Report for Marine Mammal Commission Contract No. MM5A C008. NTIS PB-289361. Springfield, Va.

21. Gibbs, J. M. 1982. *Whales off New England.* Newbury, Mass.: Gibbs and Gibbs.

22. Gurevich, V. S. 1980. "Worldwide Distribution and Migration Patterns of the White Whale (Beluga), *Delphinapterus leucas.*" *Rep. Int. Whal. Commn.* 30:465–80.

23. Hain, J. W.; R. K. Edel; H. E. Hays; S. K. Katona; and J. D. Roanowicz. 1981. "General Distribution of Cetaceans in the Continental Shelf Waters of the Northeastern United States." Chap. 2 in CETAP, *A Characterization of Marine Mammals and Turtles in the mid- and North-Atlantic Areas of the U.S. Outer Continental Shelf.* Annual Report for 1979. Cetacean and Turtle Assessment Program, Univ. Rhode Island, Kingston, RI 02881, prepared for U.S. Dept. Interior, Bureau of Land Management, 18th and C Sts., N.W., Rm. 2455, Wash., D.C. 20240.

24. Harrison, R. G. (ed.). 1972–77. *The Functional Anatomy of Marine Mammals.* Vol. 1 (1972), 451 pp.; Vol. 2 (1974), 366 pp.; Vol. 3 (1977), 428 pp. N.Y.: Academic Press.

25. ———, and J. King. 1979. *Marine Mammals.* 2nd ed. London: Hutchinson and Co. 192 pp.

26. Heintzelman, D. S. 1981. *A World Guide to Whales, Dolphins and Porpoises.* Winchester Press, P.O. Box 1260, Tulsa, OK. 156 pp.

27. Herman, L. M. (ed.). 1980. *Cetacean Behavior: Mechanisms and Functions.* N.Y.: Wiley-Interscience.

28. Hollingshead, K. W., and S. Corey. 1974. "Aspects of the Life History of *Meganyctiphanes norvegica* (*M. Sars*), Crustacea (Euphausiacea), in Passamaquoddy Bay." *Can. J. Zool.* 52:495–505.

29. International Fund for Animal Welfare. Not dated. *First Aid for Stranded Marine Mammals.* IFAW, Yarmouth Port, MA. 24 pp.

30. Jurasz, C., and V. Jurasz. 1979. "Feeding Modes of the Humpback Whale, *Megaptera novaeangliae,* in Southeast Alaska." *Sci. Rep. Whales Res. Inst.* 31:67–81.

31. Katona, S. K.; W. Steiner; and H. E. Winn. 1977. "Marine Mammals." Chap. 14 in Center for Natural Areas, *A Summary and Analysis of Environmental Information on the Continental Shelf from the Bay of Fundy to Cape Hatteras.* Vol. 1, Book 2. Bureau of Land Management, U.S. Dept. Interior. Final Report, Contract No. AA550-CT6-45.

32. ———; S. A. Testaverde; and B. Barr. 1978. "Observations on a White-Sided Dolphin, *Lagenorhynchus acutus,* Probably Killed in Gill Nets in the Gulf of Maine." *Fish. Bull.* 76(2):475–76.

33. ———; P. Harcourt; J. S. Perkins; and S. D. Kraus. 1980. *Humpback Whales. A Catalogue of Individuals Identified by Fluke Photographs.* Bar Harbor, Maine: College of the Atlantic.

34. ———, and H. P. Whitehead. 1981. "Identifying Humpback Whales Using their Natural Markings," *Polar Record* 20(128):439–44.

35. Kelly, J. E.; S. Mercer; and S. Wolf. 1981. *The Great Whale Book.* Wash., D.C.: Acropolis Books Ltd., and Center for Environmental Education, 624 9th St., N.W., Wash., D.C. 20001

36. Kraus, S. D., and J. H. Prescott. 1982. *The North Atlantic Right Whale* (Eubalaena glacialis) *in the Bay of Fundy, 1981, with Notes on Distribution, Abundance, Biology and Behavior.* Final Report for National Marine Fisheries Service Contract No. NA-81-FA-C-00030 and World Wildlife Fund, Wash., D.C.

37. Kulka, D. W., and S. Corey. 1978. "The Life History of *Thysanoessa inermis* (Kroyer) in the Bay of Fundy." *Can. J. Zool.* 56:492–506.

38. Lazell, J. D. Jr. 1976. This Broken Archipelago. N.Y.: Quadrangle Press, Harper & Row, 260 pp.

39. ———. 1980. "New England Waters: Critical Habitat for Marine Turtles." *Copeia*, 1980(2):290–95.

40. Leatherwood, S.; D. K. Caldwell; and H. E. Winn. 1976. *Whales, Dolphins and Porpoises of the Western North Atlantic: A Guide to Their Identification.* NOAA Tech. Rept. NMFS Circ. 396, U.S. Gov't. Printing Office, Wash., D.C. 176 pp.

41. Leim, A. H., and W. B. Scott. 1966. "Fishes of the Atlantic Coast of Canada." *Fish. Res. Bd. Canada Bull.* No. 155, Queen's Printer, Ottawa. 485 pp.

42. Lien, J. Not dated. "Whale Entrapment in Inshore Fishing Gear in Newfoundland." Unpub. ms. Memorial Univ. of Nfld., St. John's, Newfoundland.

43. ———, and B. Merdsoy. 1979. "The Humpback Is Not Over the Hump." *Nat. Hist.* 88(6):46–49.

44. Lockyer, C. 1976. "Estimates of Growth and Energy Budget for the Sperm Whale, Physeter catadon." United Nations Food and Agriculture Organization Scientific Consultation on Marine Mammals, Doc. ACMRR/ MM/SC/38, February 1976, Rome. 33 pp.

45. ———. 1981. "Estimation of the Energy Costs of Growth, Maintenance, and Reproduction in the Female Minke Whale (*Balaenoptera acutorostrata*), from the Southern Hemisphere." *Rep. Int. Whal. Commn.* 31:337–44.

46. MacIntyre, J. (ed.). 1974. *Mind in the Waters.* N.Y.: Charles Scribner's Sons.

47. Martin, K. R. 1975. *Whalemen and Whaleships of Maine.* Brunswick, Maine: Harpswell Press.

48. Mayo, C. A. 1982. "Observations of Cetaceans: Cape Cod Bay and Southern Stellwagen Bank, Massachusetts, 1975–1979." NTIS PB-82-186263, Springfield, Va.

49. McKay, R. S., and H. M. Liaw. 1981. "Dolphin Vocalization Mechanisms." *Science* 212:676–77.

50. Mercer, M. C. 1973. "Observations on Distribution and Intraspecific Variation in Pigmentation Patterns of Odontocete Cetacea in the Western North Atlantic." *J. Fish. Res. Bd. Canada* 30:1111–30.

51. ———. 1975. "The Interaction Between the Northern Pilot Whale (*Globicephala melaena*) and the Short-finned Squid (*Illex illecebrocus*) at Newfoundland with Particular Reference to Stock Assessments and Production Estimates." *J. Fish. Res. Bd. Canada* 32(7).

52. Meyer. T. L.; R. A. Cooper; and R. W. Langton. 1979. "Relative Abundance, Behavior, and Food Habits of the American Sand Lance, *Ammodytes americanus*, from the Gulf of Maine." *Fish. Bull.* 77(1):243–53.

53. Mitchell, E. D. 1970. "Pigmentation Pattern Evolution in Delphinid Cetaceans: An Essay in Adaptive Coloration." *Can. J. Zool.* 48(4):717–40.

54. ———. 1973. "The Status of the World's Whales." *Nature Canada* 2(4):9–27.

55. ———. 1974. "Present Status of Northwest Atlantic Fin and Other Whale Stocks." In W. E. Schevill (ed.), *The Whale Problem—a Status Report*. Cambridge, Mass.: Harvard Univ. Press, pp. 108–69.

56. ———. 1975. *Porpoise, Dolphin, and Small Whale Fisheries of the World: Status and Problems*. IUCN Monograph No. 3, Int. Union for Conservation of Nature and Natural Resources, Morges, Switzerland. 129 pp.

57. ——— (ed.). 1975. "Report of the Meeting on Smaller Cetaceans." Montreal, April 1–11, 1974. *J. Fish. Res. Bd. Canada* 32:891–945.

58. ———. 1975. "Trophic Relationships and Competition for Food in Northwest Atlantic Whales." In M. D. B. Burt (ed.), *Proceedings of the Annual Meeting of the Canadian Society of Zoology*, June 2–5, 1974. Univ. New Brunswick, Frederickton, N.B., Canada.

59. ———. 1977. "Evidence That the Northern Bottlenose Whale Is Depleted." *Rep. Int. Whal. Commn.* 27:195–203.

60. ———, and V. M. Kozicki. 1975. "Autumn Stranding of a Northern Bottlenose Whale (*Hyperoodon ampullatus*) in the Bay of Fundy, Nova Scotia." *J. Fish. Res. Bd. Canada* 32(7):1019–40.

61. ———, and V. M. Kozicki. 1975. "Supplementary Information on Minke Whale (*Balaenoptera acutorostrata*) from Newfoundland Fishery." *J. Fish. Res. Bd. Canada* 32(7):985–94.

62. ———, and D. G. Chapman. 1975. "Preliminary Assessment of N.W. Atlantic Sei Whales (*Balaenoptera borealis*)." *Rep. Int. Whal. Commn.* 25:218–25.

63. Miyazaki, N. 1977. "School Structure of *Stenella coeruleoalba*." *Rep. Int. Whal. Commn.* 27:498–99.

64. Moulton, J. M. 1963. "The Capture of a Marked Leatherback Turtle in Castro Bay, Maine." *Copeia*, 1963(2): 434–35.

65. Nemoto, T. 1970. "Feeding Pattern of Baleen Whales in the Ocean." In J. H. Steele (ed.), *Marine Food Chains*. Berkeley: Univ. California Press, pp. 241–52.

66. Nishiwaki, M. 1975. "Ecological Aspects of Smaller Cetaceans, with Emphasis on the Striped Dolphin, *Stenella coeruleoalba*." *J. Fish. Res. Bd. Canada* 32(7): 1069–72.

67. Norris, K. S. (ed.). 1966. *Whales, Dolphins and Porpoises*. Berkeley: Univ. California Press.

68. ———. 1974. *The Porpoise Watcher*. N.Y.: W. W. Norton.

69. Overholtz, W. J., and J. R. Nicolas. 1979. "Apparent Feeding by the Fin Whale, *Balaenoptera physalus*, and Humpback Whale, *Megaptera novaeangliae*, on the American Sand Lance, *Ammodytes americanus*, in the Northwest Atlantic." *Fish. Bull.* 77(1):285–87.

70. Perkins, J., and H. Whitehead. 1977. "Observations on Three Species of Baleen Whales off Newfoundland Waters." *J. Fish. Res. Bd. Canada* 34:1436–40.

71. Perkins, J. S., and P. C. Beamish. 1979. "Net Entanglements of Baleen Whales in the Inshore Fishery of Newfoundland." *J. Fish. Res. Bd. Canada* 36:521–28.

72. Pivorunas, A. 1979. "The Feeding Mechanisms of Baleen Whales." *Amer. Sci.* 67(4):432–40.

73. Powers, K. D.; P. M. Payne; and S. J. Fitch. 1982. "Marine Observer Program. Distributions of Cetaceans, Seabirds and Turtles, Cape Hatteras to Nova Scotia, June 1980–December 1981." Final report for NOAA/

NMFS Contract No. NA-81-FA-C-00023. Manomet Bird Observatory, Manomet, Mass. 02345.

74. Prescott, J. H., and P. M. Fiorelli. 1980. "Review of the Harbor Porpoise (*Phocoena phocoena*) in the Northwest Atlantic." Final report for Marine Mammal Commission Contract MM8ACO16. NTIS PB80-176 928. 64 pp.

75. ———; S. D. Kraus; P. Fiorelli; and D. E. Gaskin. 1981. "Harbor Porpoise (*Phocoena phocoena*) Distribution, Abundance, Survey Methodology and Preliminary Notes on Habitat Use and Threats." Final report to National Marine Fisheries Service, Northeast Fisheries Laboratory, Woods Hole, Mass. Unpub. ms.

76. Pryor, K. 1975. *Lads before the Wind.* N.Y.: Harper & Row.

77. Reeves, R. R.; J. G. Mead; and S. K. Katona. 1977. "The Right Whale, *Eubalaena glacialis*, in the Western North Atlantic." *Rep. Int. Whal. Comm.* 28:303–12.

78. ———, and S. K. Katona. 1980. "Extralimital records of White Whales (*Delphinapterus leucas*) in Eastern North American Waters." *Canadian Field-Nat.* 94(3)239–47.

79. Ridgway, S. H. (ed.). 1972. *Mammals of the Sea: Biology and Medicine.* Springfield, Ill.: Charles C. Thomas, Pub.

80. Scattergood, L. W., and C. Packard. 1960. "Records of Marine Turtles in Maine." *Maine Field Naturalist* 16 (3):46–50.

81. Schevill, W. E. 1956. "*Lagenorhynchus acutus* off Cape Cod." *J. Mamm.* 37:128–29.

82. ———; K. E. Moore; and W. A. Watkins. 1981. "Right Whale, *Eubalaena glacialis*, Sightings in Cape Cod Waters." Tech. Rept. WHOI-81-50. Woods Hole Oceanographic Institution, Woods Hole, Mass.

83. ——— (ed.). 1974. *The Whale Problem: A Status Report.* Cambridge, Mass.: Harvard Univ. Press.

84. Scott, F. Not dated. "The Whales, Porpoises and Dolphins of Nova Scotia." Unpub. ms., Nova Scotia Museum, Halifax, N.S.

85. Scott, G. P.; R. D. Kenny; J. P. Gilbert; and R. K. Edel.

1981. "Estimation of Cetacean and Turtle Abundance in the CETAP Study Area with an Analysis of Factors Affecting Them." Chap. 4 in *A Characterization of Marine Mammals and Turtles in the Mid- and North-Atlantic Areas of the U.S. Outer Continental Shelf.* Annual Report for 1979 for CETAP, Univ. of Rhode Island, Kingston, RI, 02881, prepared for U.S. Dept. Interior, Bureau of Land Management, 18th and C Sts., N.W., Rm. 2455, Wash., D.C. 20240.

86. Sears, R. 1982. "Cetaceans of the Gulf of St. Lawrence: Distribution and Relative Abundance." Unpub. ms., Mingan Island Cetacean Study, C.P. 159, Sept. Iles, Quebec, Canada, Feb. 1982.

87. Sergeant, D. E. 1961. "Whales and Dolphins of the Canadian East Coast." Fish. Res. Bd. Canada, Arctic Unit, Queens Printer, Ottawa, Cat. No. FS. 97-1/7, 17 pp.

88. ———. 1962. "On the External Characters of the Blackfish or Pilot Whales (genus *Globicephala*)." *J. Mammal.* 43:395–413.

89. ———. 1962. "The Biology of the Pilot or Pothead Whale *Globicephala melaena* (Traill) in Newfoundland Waters." *Fish. Res. Bd. Canada Bull.* 132. 34 pp.

90. ———. 1963. "Minke Whales, *Balaenoptera acutorostrata* Lacepede, of the Western North Atlantic." *J. Fish. Res. Bd. Canada* 20:1490–1504.

91. ———. 1966. *Populations of Large Whale Species in the Western North Atlantic with Special Reference to the Fin Whale.* Fisheries Res. Bd. Canada, Arctic Biol. Sta. Circular No. 9. 13 pp.

92. ———. 1969. "Feeding Rates of Cetacea." *Fisk. Dir. Skr. Ser. HavUnders.* 15: 246–58.

93. ———. 1974. *Ecological Isolation in Some Cetacea.* Contrib. Symp. Marine Mammals, Int. Theriological Cong., Moscow, June 6–12, 1974.

94. ———. 1977. "Stocks of Fin Whales *Balaenoptera physalus* L. in the North Atlantic Ocean." *Rep. Int. Whal. Commn.* 27:460–73.

95. ———, and P. F. Brodie. 1975. "Identity, Abundance, and Present Status of Populations of White Whale, *Del-*

phinapterus leucas, in North America." *J. Fish. Res. Bd. Canada* 32(7):1047–54.

96. Slijper, E. J. 1979. *Whales.* Ithaca, N.Y.: Cornell Univ. Press.
97. Smith, G. J. D., and D. E. Gaskin. 1974. "The Diet of Harbor Porpoises (*Phocoena phocoena* [L.]) in Coastal Waters of Eastern Canada, with Special Reference to the Bay of Fundy." *Can. J. Zool.* 52:777–82.
98. Snow, D. 1974. "The Changing Prey of Maine's Early Hunters." *Nat. Hist.* 83(11):15–24.
99. Spotte, S.; J. L. Dunn; L. E. Kezer; and F. M. Heard. 1978. "Notes on the Care of a Beach Stranded Harbor Porpoise (*Phocoena phocoena*)." *Cetology* 32:1–5.
100. Squires, H. J. 1957. "Squid, *Illex illecebrosus* (Le Sueur) in the Newfoundland Fishing Area." *J. Fish. Res. Bd. Canada* 14:693–728.
101. ———.1967. "Growth and Hypothetical Age of the Newfoundland Bait Squid *Illex illecebrosus.*" *J. Fish. Res. Bd. Canada* 24:1209–17.
102. Tomilin, A. G. 1957. *Mammals of the U.S.S.R. and Adjacent Countries.* Vol. 9, *Cetacea.* Israel Program for Scientific Translations. NTIS, Springfield, VA 22151.
103. True, F. W. 1904. *The Whalebone Whales of the Western North Atlantic Compared with Those Occurring in European Waters with Some Observations on the Species in the North Pacific.* Smithsonian Contrib. Knowl. Vol. 33, No. 1414. 332 pp.
104. Tuck, J. A., and R. Grenier. 1981. "Sixteenth Century Basque Whaling Station in Labrador." *Sci. Amer.* 245 (5):180–90.
105. Tyack, P. 1981. "Why Do Whales Sing?" *The Sciences* (N.Y. Acad. Sci.), Sept. 1981, pp. 22–25.
106. Warhol, P. 1982. "Can Odontocetes Stun Prey with Sound? The 'Big Bang' Theory. An Interview with Ken Norris." *Whalewatcher* (*J. Amer. Cetacean Soc.*) 16(2):6–8, 23.
107. Watkins, W. A. 1977. "Acoustic Behavior of Sperm Whales." *Oceanus* (Woods Hole Oceanographic Institution) 20:50–58.
108. ———. 1980. "Acoustics and the Behavior of Sperm

Whales," pp. 283–90 in R. G. Busnel and J. F. Fish (eds.), *Animal Sonar Systems*. N.Y.: Plenum Pub.

109. ———. 1981. "Activities and Underwater Sounds of Fin Whales." *Sci. Rept. Whales Res. Inst.* 33:83–118.

110. ———, and W. E. Schevill. 1979. "Aerial Observation of Feeding Behavior in Four Baleen Whales: *Eubalaena glacialis, Balaenoptera borealis, Megaptera novaeangliae,* and *Balaenoptera physalus*." *J. Mammal.* 60:155–63.

111. Watson, L. 1980. *A Sea Guide to Whales of the World*. N.Y.: E. P. Dutton.

112. Weinrich, M. T. 1982. *Biology of the Humpback Whale: Northern Stellwagen Bank, Summer 1981.* Cetacean Research Unit Special Rept. No. 1, Gloucester Fisherman's Museum, P.O. Box 159, Gloucester, MA 01930.

113. Whitehead, H. 1982. "Populations of Humpback Whales in the Northwest Atlantic." *Rep. Int. Whal. Comm.* 32:345–53.

114. ———; R. Silver; and P. Harcourt. 1982. "The Migration of Humpback Whales along the Northeast Coast of Newfoundland." *Can. J. Zool.* 60(9):2173–79.

115. Winn, H. E.; R. K. Edel; and A. G. Taruski. 1975. "Population Estimate of the Humpback Whale (*Megaptera novaeangliae*) in the West Indies by Visual and Acoustic Techniques." *J. Fish. Res. Bd. Canada* 32:499–506.

116. ———, and P. J. Perkins. 1976. "Distribution and Sounds of the Minke Whale, with a Review of Mysticete Sounds." *Cetology* 19:1–12.

117. ———, and L. K. Winn. 1978. "The Song of the Humpback Whale, *Megaptera novaeangliae,* in the West Indies." *Mar. Biol.* 47:97–114.

118. ———, and B. L. Olla (eds.). 1979. *Behavior of Marine Mammals.* Vol. 3, *Cetaceans.* N.Y.: Plenum Pub.

119. Winslade, P. 1975. "Behavioral Studies on the Lesser Sand Eel *Ammodytes marinus* (Raitt): III. The Effect of Temperature on Activity and the Environmental Control of the Annual Cycle of Activity." *J. Fish. Biol.* 6(5):587–99.

SPECIES GUIDE TO THE BIBLIOGRAPHY ON SEALS

General: 1, 2, 5, 9, 11, 12, 14, 22, 23, 26, 30, 34, 35, 36, 38, 39, 40, 41, 42
Harbor seal: 3, 8, 10, 13, 17, 33
Gray seal: 7, 13, 17, 18, 21, 24, 33
Harp seal: 4, 6, 15, 16, 37, 43
Hooded seal: 32, 43
Ringed seal: 27, 44, 45
Walrus: 19, 20, 22, 25, 28, 29, 31, 36

II. SEALS

1. Allen, J. A. 1880. *History of North American Pinnipeds.* U. S. Georgr. Surv. Terr., Misc. Publ. 12, 785 pp.
2. Backhouse, K. M. 1969. *Seals.* The World of Animals Series, N.Y.: Golden Press.
3. Boulva, J., and I. A. McLaren. 1979. "Biology of the Harbour Seal, *Phoca vitulina*, in Eastern Canada." *Bull. Fish. Res. Board Canada.* No. 200, 24 pp. Canadian Government Publishing Centre Supply and Services Canada, Hull, Quebec K1A 0S9.
4. Bruemmer, F. 1975. "A Year in the Life of a Harp Seal." *Nat. Hist.*, April 1975.
5. ———. 1972. *Encounters with Arctic Animals.* Ryerson, Toronto, and N.Y.: McGraw-Hill.
6. ———. 1977. *The Life of the Harp Seal.* N.Y.: Times Book Co.
7. Clarkson, C. 1970. *Halic: the Story of a Gray Seal.* N.Y.: Dutton.
8. Gilbert, J. R., and K. M. Wynne. 1982. *Harbor Seal Populations and Marine Mammal–Fisheries Interactions.* Annual Report to National Marine Fisheries Service. Contract No. NA-80-FC0029.
9. Gold, Joy P. (comp.). *Useful References on Seals, Sea Lions and Walruses.* Wash., D.C.: Smithsonian Institution.

10. Goodridge, H., and L. Dietz. 1975. *A Seal Called Andre.* Camden, Maine: Downeast Books.

11. Gunter, G. 1968. "The Status of Seals in the Gulf of Mexico." *Gulf Res. Rept.* 2(3):301–8.

12. Harrison, R. J. (ed.). 1968. *The Behaviour and Physiology of Pinnipeds.* N.Y.: Appleton-Century Crofts.

13. Hewer, H. R. 1974. *British Seals.* London: Collins.

14. King, J. E. 1964. *Seals of the World.* London: British Museum of Natural History.

15. Lavigne, D. M. 1976. "The Harp Seal, Past, Present and Future Considerations." *Mainstream* 7(4):18–19.

16. ———. 1976. "Life or Death for the Harp Seal." *Nat. Geogr.* 149(1):129–42.

17. Lockley, R. M. 1966. *Gray Seal, Common Seal: An Account of the Life Histories of British Seals.* London: Deutsch.

18. ———. 1955. *The Saga of the Grey Seal.* N.Y.: Devin-Adair.

19. Loughrey, A. G. 1955. *Preliminary Investigation of the Atlantic Walrus Odobenus rosmarus rosmarus (Linnaeus).* Canadian Wildlife Service, Wildlife Management Bulletin (Series 1), No. 14, 123 pp.

20. Mansfield, A. W. 1958. *The Biology of the Atlantic Walrus Odobenus rosmarus rosmarus (Linnaeus) in the Eastern Canadian Arctic.* Fisheries Research Board of Canada, Manuscript Report Series (Biological) No. 653, 146 pp.

21. ———. 1966. "The Grey Seal in Eastern Canadian Waters." *Can. Audubon Mag.* 28(4):161–66.

22. ———. 1966. "The Walrus in Canada's Arctic." *Can. Geogr. J.* 72(3):88–95.

23. ———.1967. *Seals of Artic and Eastern Canada.* Fisheries Research Board of Canada, Bulletin No. 137. Canadian Government Publishing Centre Supply and Services Canada, Hull, Quebec K1A 0S9.

24. ———, and B. Beck. 1977. *The Grey Seal in Eastern Canada.* Fish. Mar. Serv., Tech. Rept. 704, 81 pp. Available from Arctic Biological Station, Dept. of Fisheries

and the Environment, P.O. Box 400, Ste. Anne de Belle-vue, Province of Quebec.

25. Manville, R. H., and P. G. Favour, Jr. 1960. "Southern Distribution of the Atlantic Walrus." *J. Mammal.* 41(4): 499–503.

26. Maxwell, G. 1967. *Seals of the World.* World Wildlife Series 2. Boston: Houghton Mifflin.

27. McLaren, I. A. 1958. *The Biology of the Ringed Seal* (Phoca hispida Schreber) *in the Eastern Canadian Arctic.* Bull. Fish. Res. Bd. Canada, No. 118, 97 pp.

28. Miller, E. H. 1975. "Walrus Ethology. I. The Social Role of Tusks and Applications of Multidimensional Scaling." *Can. J. Zool.* 53:590–613.

29. Perry, R. 1968. *The World of the Walrus.* N.Y.: Taplinger.

30. Ray, C. 1963. "Locomotion in Pinnipeds." *Nat. Hist.* 72(3)10–21.

31. Reeves, R. R. 1978. *Atlantic Walrus* (Odobenus rosmarus rosmarus): *A Literature Survey and Status Report.* Wildlife Research Report No. 10. U.S. Dept. of the Interior, Fish and Wildlife Service, Wash., D.C.

32. Richardson, D. T. 1975. "Hooded Seal Whelps at South Brooksville, Maine." *J. Mammal.* 56(3):698–99.

33. ————. 1976. *Assessment of Harbour and Grey Seal Populations in Maine.* Maine Dept. of Mar. Res., Augusta, Maine.

34. ————; S. K. Katona; and K. Darling. 1974. "Marine Mammals." Chap 14 in *A Socio-economic and Environmental Inventory of the North Atlantic Region, Sandy Hook to Bay of Fundy.* TRIGOM (The Research Institute of the Gulf of Maine), South Portland, Maine.

35. Ridgway, S. H. (ed.). 1972. *Mammals of the Sea: Biology and Medicine.* Springfield, Ill.: Charles C. Thomas Pub.

36. ————, and R. J. Harrison (eds.). 1981. *Handbook of Marine Mammals.* Vol. 1. *The Walrus, Sea Lions, Fur Seals and Sea Otter.* Vol. 2. *Seals.* N.Y.: Academic Press.

37. Ronald, K., and J. L. Dougan. 1982. "The Ice Lover:

Biology of the Harp Seal (*Phoca groenlandica*)." *Science* 215:928–33.

38. Scheffer, V. B. 1976. *A Natural History of Marine Mammals.* N.Y.: Charles Scribner's Sons.

39. ———. 1958. *Seals, Sea Lions, and Walruses: A Review of the Pinnipedia.* Stanford: Stanford Univ. Press.

40. ———. (ed.). 1967. "Standard Measurements of Seals." *J. Mammal.* 48(3):459–62.

41. ———. 1970. *The Year of the Seal.* N.Y.: Charles Scribner's Sons.

42. Schevill, W. E.; W. A. Watkins; and C. Ray. 1963. "Underwater Sounds of Pinnipeds." *Science* 141:50–53.

43. Sergeant, D. E. 1976. "History and Present Status of Populations of Harp and Hooded Seals." *Biol. Conserv.* 10.

44. Smith, T. G. 1976. "The Icy Birthplace and Hard Life of the Arctic Ringed Seal." *Can. Geogr. J.* 93(2):58–63.

45. ———. 1973. *Population Dynamics of the Ringed Seal in the Canadian Eastern Arctic.* Bulletin No. 181, Fisheries Research Board of Canada.

46. Stuart, F. 1954. *A Seal's World.* N.Y.: McGraw-Hill.

III. PHONOGRAPH RECORDS FEATURING VOCALIZATIONS OF WHALES, DOLPHINS, AND SEALS

Callings. Paul Winter Consort. Living Music Foundation, Box 68, Litchfield, CT 06759.

Deep Voices. The second whale record. Capitol Records ST 11598.

Northern Whales. Music Gallery Editions, 30 Patrick St., Toronto, Canada M5T 1V1.

Ocean of Song: Whale Voices. PET Records, Box 1102, Burbank, CA 91507.

Songs of the Humpback Whale. Capitol Records SW 620.

Sound Communication of the Bottlenosed Dolphin. Biological System, Inc., P.O. Box 26, St. Augustine, FL 32084.

Whalescapes. Interspecies Music, Vol. 1. The Gallery, 30 Patrick St., Toronto, Ontario, Canada.

Index